AS Music
Composition Workbook

Alan Charlton
with Robert Steadman

R·
Rhinegold Education

241 Shaftesbury Avenue
London WC2H 8TF
Telephone: 020 7333 1720
Fax: 020 7333 1765

Music Study Guides

(series editor: Paul Terry)

GCSE, AS and A2 Music Study Guides (AQA, Edexcel and OCR)
GCSE, AS and A2 Music Listening Tests (AQA, Edexcel and OCR)
GCSE Music Study Guide (WJEC)
AS/A2 Music Technology Study Guide (Edexcel)
AS/A2 Music Technology Listening Tests (Edexcel)
Lifelines Revision Guides for GCSE (AQA, Edxcel and OCR), AS and A2 Music (AQA and Edexcel)
Lifelines Revision Guides AS and A2 Music Technology (Edexcel)

Also available from Rhinegold Education

Key Stage 3 Elements
Key Stage 3 Listening Tests: Book 1 and Book 2
GCSE Music Composition and Literacy Workbooks
AS Music Harmony Workbook
Baroque Music in Focus, Romanticism in Focus, Modernism in Focus
Batman in Focus, *Goldfinger* in Focus, *Immaculate Collection* in Focus, *Who's Next* in Focus
Film Music in Focus, Musicals in Focus

Rhinegold also publishes Classical Music, Classroom Music, Early Music Today, Music Teacher,
Opera Now, Piano, The Singer, Teaching Drama, British and International Music Yearbook,

British Performing Arts Yearbook, British Music Education Yearbook, Rhinegold Dictionary of Music in Sound.

Other Rhinegold Study Guides

Rhinegold publishes resources for candidates studying Classical Civilisation, Drama and Theatre Studies,
Performance Studies and Religious Studies.

First published 2008 in Great Britain by
Rhinegold Publishing Limited
239-241 Shaftesbury Avenue
London WC2H 8TF
Telephone: 020 7333 1720
Fax: 020 7333 1765
www.rhinegold.co.uk
© Rhinegold Publishing Limited 2008

Rhinegold Publishing Ltd has used its best efforts in preparing this workbook. It does not assume,
and hereby disclaims any liability to any party, for loss or damage caused by errors or omissions in the book,
whether such errors or omissions result from negligence, accident or other cause.

If you are preparing for an exam in music you should always check the current requirements of the
examination, since these may change from one year to the next.

AS Music Composition Workbook

British Library Cataloguing in Publication Data.
A catalogue record for this book is available from the British Library.
ISBN 978-1-906178-31-4
Printed in Great Britain by Headley Brothers Ltd

Contents

Authors

Alan Charlton is a composer, teacher, examiner and writer on music. He gained a PhD in composition at the University of Bristol in 1997, studying with Raymond Warren, Adrian Beaumont and Robert Saxton. His work has received numerous professional performances in the UK and abroad, and has won many prizes and awards for composition. He was the first Eileen Norris Fellow in Composition at Bedford School from 1999–2002, where he is currently head of music technology. He has taught composition to GCSE, A-level and undergraduate students, and has many years' experience as an Edexcel examiner in composition. He writes regularly for Rhinegold's *Classroom Music* and also contributed to *The Illustrated Musical Instruments Handbook* (Flame Tree 2006).

Robert Steadman is a prolific composer who has written music ranging from symphonies and operas to primary-school musicals and pieces for brass band. Among his many commissions he has written works for the percussionist Evelyn Glennie, the Royal Philharmonic Orchestra and the London Serpent Trio. He currently teaches part-time at Lady Manners School, Bakewell, as well as providing workshops and INSET on composition and music-technology topics. He has been an examiner for all the major exam boards. He writes for Rhinegold's *Classroom Music* and is the author of AQA GCSE Music Revision *Lifelines* and co-author of Revision *Lifelines* for AS and A2 Music Technology.

Acknowledgements

The authors would like to thank the series editor, Paul Terry, for his advice and suggestions. Thanks also to the Rhinegold editorial team of Chris Elcombe, Harriet Power, Sabine Wolf and Lucien Jenkins for their assistance in the editorial and production process.

Preface: using this book

What is in the book?

In this book there are five different composing projects suitable for use in AS composition coursework. As exam board specifications vary, you should discuss with your teacher which of these projects will be appropriate for the particular exam you are taking.

You are advised to follow project 1 as preparation for your coursework, as it contains general advice on writing and harmonising melodies, developing and structuring material and on writing appropriately for the instruments at your disposal. Once you have completed this project, you should follow a project of your choice from the remainder of the book for your actual coursework submission (or even follow the same project again).

Each of the projects covers two areas – a musical form (such as variations, verse-chorus song and so on) and a type of musical ensemble. In projects 1 and 3, the ensembles are general instrumental ensembles; in project 2, choirs; in project 4, rock and pop instruments; and in project 5, keyboard instruments.

Note that you do not have to stick to the instrumentation recommended for each project, and that you can combine different projects: if you want to compose a piece in variation form for solo piano, for example, you should follow the variation project but refer to project 5 for advice on piano-writing.

What is not in the book?

Most, but not all, of the composition topics set by the exam boards are covered in this book. However, there may be particular requirements of your exam board's specification that have not been covered, such as composition commentaries and working under controlled conditions. You are advised to check thoroughly with your teacher exactly what your exam board requires.

What composing experience should I have already?

This workbook assumes that you already have some experience of composing, for instance at GCSE level. If you haven't composed before, you may find it useful to familiarise yourself with the following skills before beginning a project:

1. Composing a melody and structuring it in phrases

2. Harmonising a melody with simple chords/triads

3. Developing several textures or accompaniment patterns from given chords

4. Structuring your ideas into a simple overall form (such as verse-chorus or ternary)

5. Using contrast in your music

6. Adding appropriate performance directions to your score

7. Producing a score and set of parts.

The first six of these are introduced in the starter project to the *GCSE Music Composition Workbook* (originally published as *Music Composition Workbook* Volume 1, Rhinegold 2008). Knowledge of music notation software (such as Sibelius or Finale) and sequencing software (such as Cubase or Logic) might also be helpful, but is by no means compulsory.

What other musical skills and knowledge do I need?

You should be able to read the treble and bass clefs and play an instrument to a standard whereby you can try out musical ideas. It is useful, though not essential, to be able to play a harmony instrument such as a keyboard or guitar, as this will help you work out chords and accompaniment patterns.

While many musical terms and ideas are explained in the projects themselves, or in the glossary at the back of the book, there isn't room to explain everything. For general music theory, consult a book such as the *GCSE Music Literacy Workbook* (originally published as *Music Literacy Workbook*, Rhinegold 2007) and for composing chord progressions and countermelodies, look at the *AS Music Harmony Workbook* (formerly *A Student's Guide to Harmony and Counterpoint*, Rhinegold 2008).

Can I choose the style of music I write in?

You should be able to follow the projects in any musical style you like, although some projects will suit certain styles more than others. Examples have been given in a variety of styles throughout the book to give you an idea of several of the options available. Check with your teacher that the project you choose is suitable for the style in which you would like to compose. You should also check that your chosen style conforms with the specifications of the exam board you are following.

Does my composition have to be written for actual performers to play?

This depends on the performers you have available to you and the type of music you are writing. For styles that normally involve live musicians, you will learn a good deal from working with actual performers, such as what the instruments sound like, what is practical and what works well for an ensemble. Moreover, hearing your music being performed is often a much more rewarding experience than listening to computer playback. However, for practical reasons, you may find that a performance through music software is the only way of giving an accurate account of your piece.

What method of composing should I use?

There are many different ways of composing and if you have written music before, you should have a good idea of what works well for you. The main ways are:

Note that you need to work alone: you are not able to submit group compositions.

➤ Working at an instrument, writing your ideas down on paper

➤ Working at a computer sequencer, playing your ideas into the software (be careful not to be over-reliant on notation software for the actual writing of your pieces, as composing in this way can result in very stiff-sounding rhythms and rather mechanical melodic lines)

➤ Using studio-based techniques, where you record your material track by track, improvising other ideas over it

➤ Working away from an instrument, writing your ideas onto manuscript paper.

You can of course use more than one of these methods. If you are writing for live performers, try not to write entirely at a computer: if you can, try out your music with live performers as you compose, as software can give a misleading impression of what is playable.

Project 1
Starter project: variations

If you have chosen this topic and are taking any of the following, you will need to compose your own variation theme:

➤ OCR Unit G352, Section B, Composition option (the work has to be for between four and ten instruments in this case)

➤ Edexcel Unit 2, Area of Study 1, Topic 2: Variation Structures

➤ AQA Unit 2, Brief B, Small Ensemble.

If you are taking the AQA Unit 2, Brief C, Arranging option, you will be given a specific folk song to arrange as part of the brief. This task is also likely to involve variation techniques.

Introduction

This project is based around ways of varying and developing material, one of the most important skills in composing, and takes you through the process of writing a set of variations on a theme. However, you could also use the techniques covered in this project to write any sort of piece which develops material, not just variations. If you do decide to write variations, remember that you could borrow an existing theme instead of composing one of your own, though note the warning above.

Suggested listening

- Bach: *Goldberg* Variations (keyboard) – baroque variations for a solo keyboard instrument

- Brahms: Variations on a Theme by Joseph Haydn (two pianos or orchestra) – a typical example of variations from the 19th century, with many changes of metre and key, and imaginative accompaniment textures

- Britten: Variations on a Theme of Frank Bridge (string orchestra); Nocturnal for Guitar – Britten pastiches many different styles of classical music, such as Italian opera

- Chris Brubeck: Variations on a Theme by Bach (piano, banjo, guitar, orchestra) – an example of jazz variations

- Martinů: Variations on a Slovakian Folk Song (cello and piano)

- Messiaen: *Thème et variations* (violin and piano) – variations in a 20th-century style, using added-note harmonies. Listen to the way the variation theme is played fortissimo in a very high register in the final variation to make an effective exhilarating ending

- Sor: Variations on *Ye Banks and Braes*, Op. 40 (guitar).

The theme

Step 1: composing a variation theme

You will first need to compose a theme of an appropriate length to support three minutes' worth of variations. A 16-bar melody such as the following, comprising four four-bar phrases, would work well.

You may find it easier to compose a chord pattern first and then work out a melody using that. If you decide to do this, give the chord pattern a similar structure (such as four phrases of four chords each), as it will be easier to compose a convincing melody. Refer to step 2 for more advice on chord progression.

Phrase 1 sets out the main material for the theme.

Phrase 2 moves to the dominant.

Phrase 3 rises to the highest note in the melody and descends almost to the lowest.

Phrase 4 is similar to phrase 1 but ends on the tonic note.

This melody has a clear shape (rising to the highest note in the third phrase, then descending) and strong sense of structure (four phrases of equal length). The third phrase is the most unique of the melody, whereas the first and fourth phrases are more similar. The melody comes to rest on the dominant at the halfway point.

Here is an alternative version of the melody which might not work so well:

Although this theme has the same phrase structure, its overall shape is less purposeful.

The theme is based too much around the notes of the tonic chord – G, B and D – which gives it the impression of being stuck in a rut.

Exercise 1

The first phrase of a melody has been provided on the staves below. Complete the melody, trying to achieve a balance of rising and falling movement, with a clear point of climax in the third phrase. Aim for phrases of similar length and think about the overall shape. Notes that you should aim towards in the subsequent three phrases have been included to help you.

Exercise 2

Now, on manuscript paper or at a computer, compose a 16-bar theme of your own, using a similar structure.

Step 2: harmonising the variation theme

The next stage is to devise a simple harmonisation of the theme. This will allow you to develop textures, accompaniment figures and countermelodies, and will be a good starting point for more advanced harmonic treatment later on.

Here is a simple harmonisation of the G major theme presented at the start of step 1, using common triads:

Here, tonic and dominant chords help to define the phrase structure: the first downbeat of each four-bar phrase is harmonised with a tonic chord; phrases 1 and 3 end on dominant chords (D), while phrase 2 also ends on a chord of D major, although this time this is a tonic chord of the new key as a modulation has occurred; the final phrase ends on the original tonic of G major. Other chords help to add variety, breaking up the alternating pattern of tonic and dominant chords. Compare this with the harmonisation on the next page.

This is a less successful harmonisation of the theme. There are fewer chords used, so the music is less harmonically interesting, and tonic and dominant chords are used a little arbitrarily – for example, in bars 7–8, the C♯ in the melody and the A major chord prepare a modulation to the dominant (D), but a G major chord is used in bar 8 instead of a D major chord. This arbitrary chord selection, and the repetition of chords such as in bars 11–13, weakens the flow of the melody.

Exercise 3

Now harmonise your own theme. Remember, you do not have to have the same number of chords in each bar. You may find that some bars work best with one chord, others with two or more. Look for triads that share one or two notes with the melody in that bar. There will be more than one triad that will work in each situation, so you will have to juggle them around to find the most satisfying progression. If no single chord works for a whole bar, try inserting extra chords. If you find that the chord progression seems a little directionless, try substituting alternative chords and substituting first-inversion chords for root-position ones.

Note that, before you can use your harmonised melody as an actual theme, you will probably need to respace the chords, create a suitable texture for it, and score it for an ensemble. Further advice on harmonisation can be found on page 16 of this chapter. For more on understanding harmony and inversions, refer to the *AS Music Harmony Workbook* by Hugh Benham (Rhinegold 2008).

Varying the theme

Let's assume you now have a complete variation theme, consisting of a melody and a simple harmonisation. What features of this theme could you change in a subsequent set of variations?

➢ Rhythm

➢ Melody

➢ Harmony

➢ Tonality

➢ Texture

➢ Instrumentation or timbre

➢ Tempo

➢ Performance directions, such as dynamics and phrasing.

Of course, more than one of these changes could be applied at the same time, and in fact, it is rare for a variation to change just one of these features.

Step 3: exploring rhythmic change

A theme can be changed by giving it a new rhythm. The example below shows several ways of varying the first phrase of our theme. Notice how, in rhythms 1–4, the rhythmic pattern established in the first full bar of each example forms the basis of the rhythm for the subsequent bars.

Rhythm 1 creates a Scottish feel by using a Scotch-snap (or lombardic) rhythm on the first beat of every bar.

Rhythm 2 uses off-beat notes and rests to create a breathless quality.

Rhythm 3 is in 𝄴 time and has a syncopated rhythm.

Rhythm 4 uses repeated notes that suggest a fanfare-like idea, perhaps suitable for a trumpet.

Rhythm 5 however, has no regular pattern and, although there is plenty of variety, the result is a little purposeless. This type of idea can often result if an attempt is made to make the rhythm more interesting without really thinking about the end result.

Exercise 4

Compose four versions of the first phrase of your melody, each with different rhythmic qualities, referring to the examples above. Try to include a dotted rhythm, a syncopated rhythm and a rhythm in a different metre.

Of course, it is not just melodies whose rhythms may be altered. Accompaniments, countermelodies and percussion parts can be added to a melody to give a new overall rhythmic effect, or to reinforce what is already there. Here are some possibilities:

In **rhythm 6**, the melody and rhythmic accompaniment interact well, with one part moving when the other is still.

In **rhythm 7**, the accompaniment repeats a single rhythm as an ostinato, while the melody has its own independent rhythm.

In **rhythm 8**, the melody and accompaniment have the same rhythm. This can produce a striking effect, particularly when it follows a more complex rhythmic texture.

In **rhythm 9**, the melody and accompaniment interact poorly with each other, the overall effect sounding less well defined than in the other examples.

Exercise 5

Compose an accompaniment rhythm to one of the melodies you produced in exercise 4.

Stretching and compressing rhythms is another useful way of developing material:

Rhythm 10 doubles each note value of the original melody (augmentation).

Rhythm 11 halves each note value of the original melody (diminution).

Rhythm 12 removes or inserts short note values into the original rhythm in an irregular way, producing changing stress patterns.

Rhythm 13 is a version of the melody in irregular metres.

Notice how, in rhythms 10-12, the stress patterns of the original melody are changed, giving the melody a new shape and feel.

Exercise 6

Write down two new versions of your theme, each using one of the above techniques.

Step 4: exploring melodic change

So far we have looked at ways of changing only the rhythm of melodies. You can of course also change the pitches of a melody and insert new ones too. There are many different methods of varying the notes of a melody, of which the following are just a few:

Melody 3

Melody 4

Melody 5

Melody 6

Melody 7

In **melody 1**, some notes have been moved up or down an octave: this gives the melody a different, very angular character.

In **melody 2**, the leaps in the melodic line have been expanded.

In **melody 3**, the melody has been inverted: upward leaps are substituted for downward ones and vice versa.

In **melody 4**, passing notes have been added to fill in the leaps in the melody line.

In **melody 5**, melodic decorations – written-out turns, mordents and appoggiaturas – have been added.

In **melody 6**, scalic figuration has been created around the melody notes (notice also the transposition by an octave of the third and fourth notes of the theme – this creates a run of notes that has more direction).

In **melody 7**, arpeggio figuration has been created around the melody notes (as in melody 6, there is some flexibility regarding the original notes of the theme, to allow more convincingly shaped arpeggiation to be used).

Exercise 7

Compose three different versions of the first phrase of your theme, each using one of the techniques described above.

Step 5: exploring harmonic variety

Another way of developing material is to modify the harmony. Let's assume that the theme we have chosen already has a harmonisation, based on triads formed from the notes of the theme's home key. Here are several different suggestions as to how to elaborate or change this harmonisation:

In **harmonisation 1**, extra chords have been added between the chords of the original harmonisation. This increases the harmonic movement, giving the music more impetus.

In **harmonisation 2**, the chords in the accompaniment are more complex, with the use of a tonic pedal note, chromaticism, augmented triads and 7th chords.

For more help with understanding how harmony works, see the *AS Music Harmony Workbook* by Hugh Benham (Rhinegold 2008).

Harmonisation 3 uses two pedal notes a 5th apart in the bass, with added-note chords above them formed from the notes of the G major scale.

If you can, play through these examples, listen to someone else doing so, or sequence them using software. How are the moods of the three harmonisations different?

> **Exercise 8**
>
> Compose two alternative harmonisations of the first phrase of the theme you created in exercise 3, perhaps using some of the above techniques. Complete one of these for the whole theme.

Harmonic writing is a complex skill that is best learnt through experience. Be prepared to try out lots of different possibilities until you find something that works well. While it is not possible in a book of this size to give detailed advice, here are a few general points that may help you:

➤ Try to give the bass line a melodic shape that is different to that of the melody: contrary motion tends to work well

➤ If the inner parts in a chord progression move by step, the progression tends to sound more purposeful

➤ Try not to overuse a single chord or chord progression: in the progression of C – G – C – G, C – C – G – G, could you use F, Dm⁷ or Am instead of one of the C chords?

➤ Make sure that the harmonies, especially at the beginnings and endings of phrases, make sense, since this will help to convey a clear structure and give the music a sense of purpose

➤ Vary the type of harmonisation across a piece – a melody could appear with just a pedal note, with a second part in counterpoint or even unaccompanied, as well as with a chord-based accompaniment.

Step 6: exploring textural variety

By now, you should have produced several possible ideas that could be developed into individual variations. Another important way to give character to a variation is the use of texture – the way in which the melody, bass and accompaniment relate to each other. Rushing scales are a type of texture, as are tune-and-accompaniment, an Alberti bass line, counterpoint and a jazz solo in stop time. Textures are a very important way of providing variety in a piece and help sustain the musical interest over a long period of time.

Let's look at how some of the ideas from earlier on can be adapted into different types of texture.

Texture 1: two-part texture based on scales (simple harmonisation) ♩=120

Texture 2: two parts answering each other (harmonisation 1) ♩=100

Texture 3: repeated chords (harmonisation 2) ♩ = 74

Texture 4: broken chords over a rhythmic ostinato (harmonisation 3) ♩=74

Texture 1 is based on the scalic idea in melody 6. A series of five-note scales has been added in the bass part: each of these outlines the notes of the chords of the simple harmonisation (G major and D major), which is enough to give the passage some harmonic direction.

Texture 2 is based on rhythm 6. A second part has been added underneath the melody that is based on the notes of harmonisation 1.

Texture 3 uses the chords of harmonisation 2, placing them on off-beats to create a more interesting rhythm.

Texture 4 is derived from harmonisation 3. The chords in the top part have been changed into broken chords.

> It is important to think about tempo, dynamics and phrasing at this stage, as these are an essential part of a musical idea's character.

Let's compare these ideas with three textures that work less well. Why might the following examples not be as effective as the previous ones?

Texture 5

Texture 6

Texture 7

In **texture 5**, the chords are too thickly spaced to be effective – the music sounds muddy and indistinct. However, it could be made to work if orchestrated well, or simply moved to a higher register.

In **texture 6**, the problem is the lack of consistency in the accompaniment. Although the harmonisation works, the lack of any pattern to the rhythm means that it comes across as forced and unnatural. Of course, there may be times when this sort of effect is desirable.

In **texture 7**, lumpiness is the main issue: the accompaniment rhythm does not help the melody to flow, stalling in bars 2 and 4. This gives the passage a stop-start feel.

All three of these textures have too much emphasis on the main beats of the bar and are typical of ideas that can result from using notation software without really thinking about what you are writing.

Exercise 9

Create three contrasting textures from material you have invented so far. You can base them on the examples of textures used above, or invent your own.

The instruments

Considering orchestration and timbre

Orchestration, or the way music is scored for instruments, is a vital tool in establishing how the music is put across to the listener. If used well, it can also help the listener hear aspects of the music such as phrase structure and the beginnings of new sections. Careful use of the range of tone colours available and of the various ways in which they can be combined can produce attractive and striking timbres, adding another layer of interest to a composition. However, orchestration also needs to be practical: you need to consider the abilities of your musicians, and what you can and cannot write for those instruments.

Step 7: choosing your ensemble

There are several factors to bear in mind when choosing an ensemble. First of all, what players are available to you? You need not write for those players only, but it will help you immensely to hear your ideas played on real instruments, in order to find out both whether they are practical and whether they produce the sounds you want.

The players available to me are:

....

....

....

Secondly, what sort of ensemble will best convey the style of the music you envisage writing? For instance, if you are writing in a pop/rock idiom, rock instruments will be more suitable than classical ones.

The intended style of my music is:

....

Thirdly, the exam board may specify the number of players you are allowed to use, so remember to check this with your teacher before you make any decisions

Different types of ensemble

A **solo harmony instrument**, such as piano, guitar or organ can give you a wide range of textures. The instrument would play both melody and accompaniment, so is self-sufficient.

Adding a melody instrument (such as violin, trumpet or lead guitar) to the harmony instrument can provide more flexibility and colour. You can add a second melody instrument to provide further colour. You could also **add a bass instrument** (such as cello, double bass or bass guitar), which will give you further textural options such as allowing you to pass melodies between separate treble and bass instruments, and to explore more melodic bass lines. In jazz and pop music the ensemble would be further enlarged by **adding a drum kit**, enabling an independent rhythm part to be added.

Another type of group is an **ensemble of broadly similar melody instruments**, such as a string quartet, clarinet quartet, brass quintet or wind quintet. Here, the instruments are well matched and cover different registers from low to high, allowing the spacing and register of textures to be varied. If you do not have the right instruments, you could substitute others with a similar register and volume, and still maintain a balanced ensemble (for instance, substituting an oboe or flute for the first violin in a string quartet).

Mixed ensembles are composed of more diverse instruments (a common one is flute, clarinet, violin, cello, piano and percussion, as used in Peter Maxwell Davies' *Ave maris stella*. These offer you a large amount of textural and timbral variety and are particularly effective when you start contrasting different instrumental combinations within the ensemble.

Now choose your ensemble. Make sure that the group will be able to play melodies and accompaniments in different registers and that the instruments can blend well together.

> The instruments in my chosen ensemble are:
>
> ....
>
> ....

Step 8: finding out more about the instruments

It is a good idea to research your instruments so that you can exploit their capabilities to the full. If you have a particular performer in mind, find out what they can do on their instrument, as every player has different strengths. You also need to know which clef(s) the instrument uses and whether it is a transposing instrument. Guitars and double basses, for example, sound an octave lower than written. Can the instrument produce any alternative timbres or effects (such as pizzicato on the violin or using a mute on the trumpet)?

For more information on instrumental techniques, see pages 56–59 of the *GCSE Music Composition Workbook* by Alan Charlton (Rhinegold 2008). The book *Orchestral Technique* by British composer Gordon Jacob (OUP 1982) is another good source to refer to. As the title suggests, it only deals with writing for orchestra but it is full of good advice.

When you have found out the ranges of your chosen instruments, as well as the sorts of effects they can produce (given the particular performers you are working with), write the details down in the table below.

Instrument name	Clef used	Lowest note	Highest note	Effects available

Exercise 10

Below are some examples of instrumental writing that are either impossible or very hard to play. Can you work out why? (Answers are provided at the end of the chapter.)

Reasons for difficulty in performance:

1. ....
2. ....
3. ....
4. ....
5. ....
6. ....
7. ....
8. ....

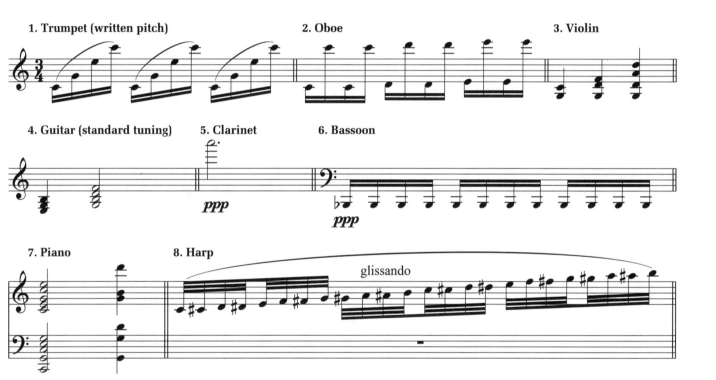

When you are writing for the instruments in your ensemble, be especially careful not to fall into traps like these.

Step 9: adapting textures for your chosen ensemble

It is likely that the ideas you have produced so far will need some modification in order to work well with your ensemble. Here are some questions for you to consider:

➢ Does the music fit within the ranges of the ensemble?

➢ Will wind and brass players have enough time to breathe?

➢ Would the instruments sound better in a different register?

➢ Might some instruments be too prominent in the texture?

➢ Does the texture need thickening, thinning or respacing?

Here are some examples of the sorts of modifications you might need to make. Three of the textures from earlier in the chapter have been scored for different ensembles. What changes have been made, and why?

Texture 1 has been arranged for clarinet quartet, with the upper stave shared between two clarinets. This solves any breathing problems that would have occurred had the line been written for a single clarinet. Notice that the end of each player's phrase overlaps with the beginning of that of the other player. This produces a smoother join between the phrases. The bottom line has been shared between clarinet 3 and the bass clarinet, adding interest by creating a dialogue between them.

Texture 3 has been rewritten for string quartet. This particular scoring, with soft trills and tremolos, helps to create an intimate mood. The cello's off-beat rhythm creates a pulsing effect which keeps the passage moving.

Texture 4 has been rearranged for guitar trio. The semiquaver broken chords have been shared between the guitars so that all the notes are sustained. This creates a similar effect to holding the sustaining pedal down on a piano, creating a richer sound. Note that this passage will sound an octave lower than written.

Exercise 11

Arrange two of your textures for your chosen ensemble, adapting your material as necessary.

Putting it all together

Step 10: structuring your piece

Writing a theme and variations will not by itself guarantee a successful musical structure. Although variation form is itself a structure, the way the variations follow on from each other, how they are contrasted and the overall shape of the piece are important to the music's success. Having written or chosen a theme, and developed several melodic, rhythmic, harmonic and textural ideas, you should now look at how you can build a convincing structure based around these ideas.

First, calculate how many variations you will need. Check with your teacher how many minutes of music the exam board specifies (probably around three). Time your theme and see how many variations you will need to fill up the requisite length of time. (You might need to adjust this calculation if you are planning to incorporate any tempo changes into your piece.)

Total length required: ...... minutes ...... seconds

Length of theme: .... seconds

Number of additional variations required: ....

Next, decide how you would like your composition to end. Here are some ideas for a final variation:

➤ A triumphant, loud variation for the whole ensemble, at a stately tempo

➤ A dazzling, virtuoso variation

➤ A dance-like variation, perhaps in §

➤ A quiet, tranquil variation

➤ A melodramatic, tragic ending, in a minor key (probably the tonic minor of the key of the theme)

➤ A light-hearted joke ending – perhaps a parody of the theme in a popular style.

> Describe your intended final variation:
>
> ....
> ....

Now that you know how your composition begins and ends, you can work on an overall shape. This shape might involve the theme progressively evolving, or it might contain strong contrasts from variation to variation. Some common shapes to consider are:

➢ Starting simply, becoming more and more complex harmonically, melodically and rhythmically

➢ Starting slowly, getting faster and faster

➢ Starting quietly, getting louder and louder

➢ Moving through a range of related styles which become more and more extrovert – for example, Latin-American forms, pastiches of different composers, a journey through selected jazz or popular-music styles

➢ Alternating contrasting variation types, such as fast and slow, major and minor, chordal and contrapuntal.

Think of the variations as a series of different moods, events, objects, people, countries, historical periods or living things. Some examples are suggested below.

Adjectives	Sad, happy, angry, strange, humorous, solemn, hyperactive, triumphant
Animals	Sloth, lion, meerkat, rabbit, snake, frog, elephant
Famous people	Sir Alan Sugar, Amy Winehouse, Andy Murray, Ricky Gervais, Brian Sewell, the Queen

Now write out a brief description of the character of each of your variations (perhaps just a word or two for each). There is no need to fill in all the boxes: only include the number of variations you will actually need.

Theme	Var 1	Var 2	Var 3	Var 4	Var 5	Var 6

Some suggested final structures are shown at the end of step 11.

Step 11: planning individual variations in more detail

It is important that your variations contrast effectively with one another: one of the common failings of variation-form pieces is that the variations sound too similar. Apart from contrasts of melody, rhythm, harmony, texture and orchestration, there are several other ways of differentiating your variations.

> You also need to make sure that all your variations belong together in the same piece: see step 12 for more advice.

Tonal contrast

It is a good idea to include some contrasts of key, with perhaps two or more different keys besides the tonic. Common keys to use are the tonic minor, relative minor/major, dominant and subdominant, but you might find it more interesting to use more remote keys. If your theme is in C major, for instance, you could think of using A♭ major, E major or F♯ minor. Whatever keys you pick, try to arrange them in a shape that goes from the home key to increasingly remote keys, but ends back where it started.

Here are some examples of possible tonal schemes:

➢ G major – E minor – D major – G major

➢ C major – C minor – A♭ major – C♯ minor – C major.

Because there is a natural ending to each variation, you might find that there is no need for a formal modulation, and that you can just start in the new key without any preparation. If this seems like too much of a jolt, try a different key or look at the section on smoothing joins between variations on the next page.

Contrasts of tempo

This is a very effective way of producing contrast. Think about increasing the tempo of the livelier variations and reducing the speed of the more sedate or sombre ones. Ending with either a stately or fast-and-furious tempo for the final variation can help create an effective climax to the piece.

Dynamic contrast

Again, this is a simple but very effective way of contrasting variations. You can reinforce dynamic changes through the scoring: for example, try using tutti for very loud passages and only a few instruments for quiet sections, although using the whole ensemble at pianissimo or just a few instruments at forte can also be very effective.

Metrical contrast

This has already been touched upon under rhythm, but remember that rewriting, say, a passage as a § one is a very good way of creating a complete change of mood.

Refer back to your overall shape that you devised in step 10 and plan in detail what will happen in each variation. If you have produced a list of words, think how you would illustrate each word musically. For instance, if you chose 'elephant', the tempo might be slow, the dynamic loud, the instrumentation quite thick and the register fairly low, perhaps with the theme in the bass. Write out a table like the following (an imaginary variation piece on famous people for flute (fl), clarinet (cl), violin (vn), cello (vc) and piano (pf)) to help you structure your variations. Note that the purpose of this is to give yourself clear starting points for individual variations: you can always change the details when you come to compose them.

	Theme	Var 1	Var 2	Var 3	Var 4
Person	Sir Alan Sugar	Paula Radcliffe	Amy Winehouse	Ricky Gervais	The Queen
Key	G maj	G maj	E min	D maj	G maj
Tempo	Allegretto	Presto	Largo	Vivace	Maestoso
Dynamic	*p*	*pp* but *mf* for third phrase	*mf*	*f* alternating with *p*	*f*, ending *ff*
Metre	¾	²/₄	¾	§/₈	4/4
Instrumentation	tutti	fl and cl alternating with vn and vc	vn, vc, pf but fl, cl, pf for 3rd phrase	fl, cl, vn, vc playing accompaniment; pf playing tune in 8ves	tutti
Possible ideas	tune and companiment; assured, confident	antiphonal, staccato; short, nervous phrases	sustained, legato; expressive, sad	rustic and dance-like; boisterous energetic, humorous	homophonic; majestic, noble-sounding

Step 12: completing the variations

You are now ready to work on composing the variations themselves. Your main aim at this stage should be to give a strong individual character to each variation that is obviously different from all the other variations you have written, yet still fits in with the piece as a whole.

To achieve this, you should be thinking of developing two or three musical features out of melody, rhythm and harmony in each variation. Each variation should have its own texture and if possible a different style of instrumentation. Also consider changes in register, key, tempo, dynamics and metre when beginning each variation.

Smoothing joins between variations

A drawback of variation form is that it can have an unwanted stop-start feel to it in the places where one variation ends and the next one begins. Where the change seems too abrupt, you might want to smooth the join in one of the following ways:

Method 1: keeping movement going at the cadence

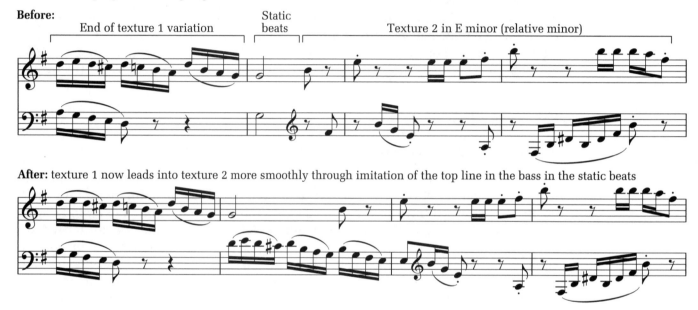

Method 2: inserting a transition passage

Before:

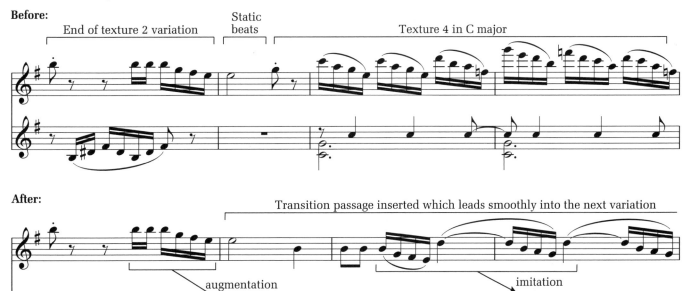

After:

However, you might find that, in some cases, having a natural moment of rest between variations works very well, so use your judgement in deciding whether or not to smooth over a join.

As your composition progresses, play or listen to all of the music you have written from start to finish at regular intervals to check that it makes sense as a piece of music. If certain parts seem dull or repetitive, think about how you could alter them to provide more interest. Could you make the rhythm more exciting, develop the texture more imaginatively or modify the harmony?

On the other hand, if certain sections sound rather out of place, try adapting them so they fit in more with the surrounding music. You could simplify the rhythm or harmony, try out different keys, or swap variations around so there is not so much of a jolt.

If an individual variation seems lacking in interest, try doing something different in its third phrase, such as changing the instrumentation, texture, register or dynamic. A simple change such as having a sudden pianissimo, changing the melody instrument, changing from legato to staccato or removing the bass line, can be very effective.

Devising an effective ending

It is important to try to round off your variations with a convincing ending. An easy way to do this is to repeat the last phrase at a slower tempo, loudly, ending on a held tonic chord. You could also make the chords thicker, expand the register by doubling the top line an octave lower and the bass line an octave lower, and perhaps use trills and tremolandi to make the texture sound more thrilling. A subtler ending might be for the music to peter out, removing instruments one by one until just one is left. Listen to some actual variation-form pieces for more ideas on endings.

Step 13: the finishing touches

To ensure that your performers play your music in the way that you want them to, it is very important to add performance details, including tempo markings, dynamics, articulation, phrasing and technical marks such as bowing. Hopefully, you should already have a fair amount of detail: you should try to get into the habit of writing down performance marks when you first compose your ideas. The main rule here is that the markings should be both meaningful and consistent. Never put in markings without thinking about them first, as the chances are that they will not make sense.

Some markings mean different things depending on the instrument reading them: some players may interpret a phrase mark as a slur, for instance. Make sure you are aware of these differences. Here are some common markings to be found in string and wind parts:

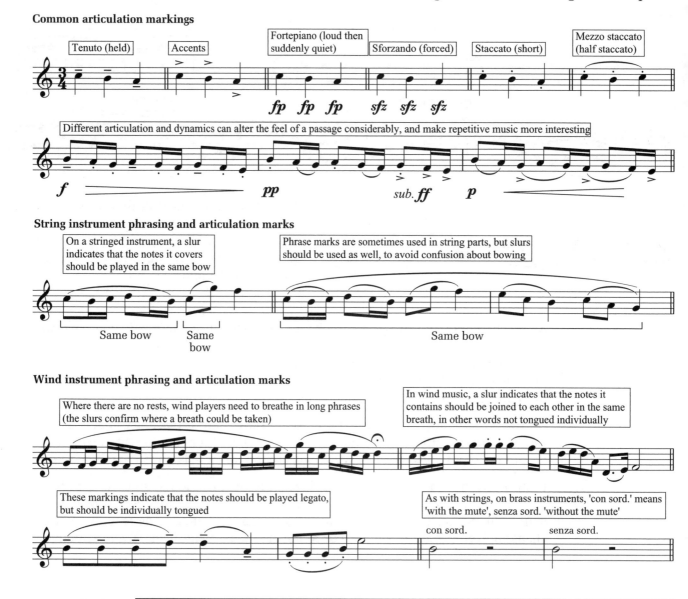

Common articulation markings

String instrument phrasing and articulation marks

Wind instrument phrasing and articulation marks

Answers to exercise 10

1 and 2. Fast passages containing wide leaps are generally very awkward for brass and wind instruments.

3 and 4. These chords are impossible to play.

5. It is very hard to play quietly this high up.

6. The bottom note of the bassoon is very hard to play quietly.

7. Chords impossible without spreading them.

8. Harp can only play seven notes to an octave without changing pedals.

Project 2
Composing for choir

This project should be suitable for Edexcel candidates who have chosen AS Unit 2, Area of Study 2 (Vocal Music), topics 3 and 4, and AQA candidates taking AS Unit 2 Brief C: Arranging. However, you are also advised to check your exam board's specification for confirmation that this is an appropriate project for you to select.

Introduction

The choir is one of the oldest types of musical ensemble and comes in many different forms, including church choirs, chamber choirs, choral societies, gospel choirs, male-voice choirs, close harmony groups, children's choirs, and choirs performing traditional and world music.

Suggested listening

- Bach: *Goldberg* Variations (keyboard) – baroque variations for a solo keyboard instrument
- Brahms: Variations on a Theme by Joseph Haydn (two pianos or orchestra) – a typical example of variations from the 19th century, with many changes of metre and key, and imaginative accompaniment textures
- Britten: Variations on a Theme of Frank Bridge (string orchestra); Nocturnal for Guitar – Britten pastiches many different styles of classical music, such as Italian opera
- Chris Brubeck: Variations on a Theme by Bach (piano, banjo, guitar, orchestra) – an example of jazz variations
- Martinů: Variations on a Slovakian Folk Song (cello and piano)
- Messiaen: *Thème et variations* (violin and piano) – variations in a 20th-century style, using added-note harmonies. Listen to the way the variation theme is played fortissimo in a very high register in the final variation to make an effective exhilarating ending
- Sor: Variations on *Ye Banks and Braes*, Op. 40 (guitar).

A conventional choir has four different parts. The top two lines are usually sung by women's voices, with sopranos taking the top line and altos the second highest. The bottom two lines are taken by men, with tenors singing the higher of these and the basses singing the lowest part. In some choirs, the top line may be taken by children's voices (sometimes referred to as trebles) and the alto line by men singing falsetto. The approximate comfortable ranges of the different voices are as follows:

> Although a lot of music is for four-part (SATB) choir, you can choose to write for other types of choir if you wish. If you do so, make sure to research which voices the choir contains and be aware of any other performance-related issues.

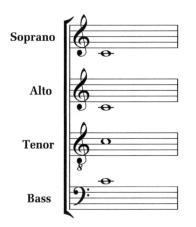

Soprano

Alto

Tenor

Bass

In practice, voices can go a few notes higher and/or lower than these, so you do not have to stick rigidly to these limits. Four-part choral music is usually written on four staves, with the soprano and alto using the treble clef, the tenor also using the treble clef but sounding an octave lower (note the '8' written below the tenor's clef symbol in the example on the right), and the bass using the bass clef.

Although choral music is often in four parts, it is also possible for these parts to divide. Therefore, unless you are writing for solo voices, you need not be restricted to using only four parts. You can also use solo voices from within the choir.

> Thomas Tallis' motet, *Spem in alium,* is famously written for 40 different parts, but it is unusual to find pieces of more than eight parts.

Choirs are capable of a wide range of dynamics. Generally speaking, loud sounds are most easily produced in the middle-to-upper range of the voice, while quiet sounds are most comfortable in the middle-to-lower range (see step 12 for more advice on writing practically and sympathetically for singers). In addition to singing, choirs can produce a variety of other sounds, including speaking, whispering, shouting, whispering, finger clicking, hand claps and so on.

To give you an idea of what choirs can do, listen to a range of choral music from different traditions. This will help you to make a decision about the sort of choral music you would like to write.

The text

Step 1: choosing your text

This is the first stage in composing a choral piece, unless you have already been given a text to set, in which case you can continue to step 2. You may have been given a general theme for the music (such as 'nature'), an occasion at which the piece will be performed (such as a church service) or a certain type of choir (chamber choir, gospel choir, close-harmony group), any of which will help you narrow down the possibilities.

The first thing to consider is how long the piece needs to be. This will give you an idea of the amount of text you need. As a general rule of thumb, a musical setting of a text will take at least three times the length of time it takes to read out the text, so for a three-minute piece, you should be aiming for text that takes between 30 seconds to a minute to read.

You also need to think about whether the structure of your text will fit in with a musical structure. For instance, if you want to write a conventional melody in four phrases, you should look at poems with four- or eight-line verses.

Texts for special occasions

Search the internet using appropriate search terms. For example, if you are looking for birthday texts, you could try 'birthday poems', 'birthday poetry', 'birthday ode', 'birthday music', 'birthday choral music', 'birthday choral programmes' and so on.

Texts for worship

Music has always played an important role in the Christian church, so it is not surprising that a vast amount of western choral music uses religious texts. Common genres of choral composition

> Although copyright lasts for 70 years after the death of the copyright holder (usually the author/composer), you do not need to seek permission to use a poem/lyric if it is only to be used in an examination submission. If, however, you intend it to be performed in a concert or recorded for any other purpose (including school concerts), then you do need permission. You will usually need to contact the publishers of the text to secure this.

include the mass, requiem mass, vespers, psalms, hymns, carols, motets and anthems. You can find appropriate texts through internet searches, or by looking through books such as the Bible and the Book of Common Prayer. For Hindu texts, look at the Rigveda and for Jewish texts, piyyutim and zemirot (Jewish hymns) and pizmonim (Hebrew songs) are good sources of text. Buddhist chants can be found in the Pali canon, while for Islamic texts, investigate Sufi poetry and the tradition of Qasidah. Be aware, however, that it may be inappropriate to set certain religious texts to music, so if you think this might be a problem, do check your choice of text with someone who can tell you what the conventions are.

You could also find texts by looking through other composers' worklists (again, searchable on the internet), or looking through collections of choral music, such as carol or motet anthologies, or hymn books. You could also consider setting foreign languages, such as Latin texts.

Poetry

This option gives you the most freedom as there is a vast amount of poetry from which to choose. Common themes in poetry are nature and landscape, myths, war, comedy, and personal feelings such as love, loss and desire. There is so much to choose from, but you can narrow it down in the following ways:

➢ Choose a particular topic, such as the sea

➢ Choose a particular era of poetry, such as the 20th century

➢ Choose a particular poet, for example Gerard Manley Hopkins.

You could then look in relevant poetry anthologies (such as anthologies of 20th-century verse, war poetry and so on), or search the internet for 'sea poetry', '20th-century poems' and so on.

Here are some suggested poems, which cover a range of themes:

➢ *The Evening Darkens Over* (Robert Bridges) – landscape/pastoral

➢ *Tall Nettles* (Edward Thomas) – landscape/pastoral

➢ *Music, When Soft Voices Die* (Percy Bysshe Shelley) – memory/the senses/love and death

➢ *Jolly Good Ale and Old* (William Stevenson) – food and drink

➢ *Love is a Sickness Full of Woes* (Samuel Daniel) – love

➢ *Requiem* (Robert Louis Stevenson) – death

➢ *Beat! Beat! Drums* (Walt Whitman) – war

➢ *To Germany* (Charles H. Sorley) – war.

Step 2: planning the structure of your piece

The structure of your composition will depend very much on the text you have chosen. Does it have an obvious overall structure?

Let's look at *The Evening Darkens Over* by Robert Bridges:

The evening darkens over After a day so bright, The windcapt waves discover That wild will be the night. There's sound of distant thunder.	The latest sea-birds hover Along the cliff's sheer height; As in the memory wander Last flutterings of delight, White wings lost on the white.	There's not a ship in sight; And as the sun goes under, Thick clouds conspire to cover The moon that should rise yonder. Thou art alone, fond lover.

As you can see, this poem is in three verses. This might suggest a strophic musical structure (using the same music for each verse) in three parts, with each verse having a different mood. Alternatively, a ternary-form structure (ABA) might work well, with the first and third verses using similar material and the second providing contrast. Since there are many striking images in the text, another possibility is a through-composed setting, where the music responds to the mood of the text.

Texts do not always have as clear a structure as this. If your text appears not to have an obvious structure, you could consider a through-composed setting. However, it is a still a good idea to break it down into sections, which might be the ends of sentences or places where there are changes of theme, mood or perspective. Remember, you can always repeat chunks of the text, such as by bringing back the opening line of the poem at the end.

Verse-chorus and rondo structures are other options worth considering if your poem has a chorus or a repeated line at the end of each verse.

The structure of my chosen poem is:

....

....

A musical structure that would reflect this is:

....

....

Step 3: interpreting the text

It is important that you understand what your poem is about so that you can set an appropriate mood and highlight the important parts of the poem in your music.

The Evening Darkens Over is an account of how images that have been visible (such as seagulls flying against a white cliff) become obscured and fade from the memory as night descends and a storm brews. The last line, 'Thou art alone, fond lover', reveals that the description of these fading images could be a metaphor for the writer's experience of being separated from his lover. Both the image of the lover and the intensity of the relationship fade from the writer's consciousness to be replaced by emotional turmoil (represented by the thunder and the hidden moon).

How will this interpretation help when setting the poem to music? It gives an idea of an appropriate mood, which might be fairly despondent, perhaps in a minor key, using a low register and descending melodic lines. This could be contrasted with brighter musical moments, such as major harmonies and higher registers, to accompany more optimistic images in the poem ('day so bright', 'the sun' and 'mood should rise').

It is also clear that the last line, 'Thou art alone, fond lover', is the most important of the poem, as up to that point the poem has just been a description of a darkening landscape. Therefore, it would be good to highlight this musically in a way that will provide a contrast to the rest of the composition. If most of the setting is in harmony for instance, setting the final line in unison might work well here.

Write out a brief interpretation of your poem, then suggest ways in which this interpretation could influence the music. What is the general mood of the poem? How might this affect aspects of the music such as tempo and key? Are there any particularly important phrases in the poem? How could you highlight these musically?

Step 4: establishing the stress patterns of the text

All words are constructed from one or more single sounds, or syllables. If you say a long word slowly, such as 'interpretation', you can hear the syllables clearly: 'In-ter-pre-ta-tion'. Some syllables are stressed more strongly than others, so 'ter' and 'ta' in 'interpretation' are emphasised

> If you are following AQA brief C, you can skip this step.

more than 'in', 'pre' and 'tion'. From this pattern of stressed and unstressed syllables you can create a musical rhythm which you can then develop into a melody in the following way.

First, go through the text, underlining each syllable that would be emphasised when spoken, as in the following example:

The <u>eve</u>ning <u>dark</u>ens <u>o</u>ver
<u>Af</u>ter a <u>day</u> so <u>bright</u>,
The <u>wind</u>capt <u>waves</u> dis<u>co</u>ver
That <u>wild</u> will <u>be</u> the <u>night</u>.
There's <u>sound</u> of <u>distant</u> <u>thunder</u>.

Next, choose a musical metre and compose a rhythm to fit the words, aiming for the underlined syllables to fall on strong beats, such as the first and third beat in 4/4 or the first and fourth quavers in 6/8. Here are two versions of the above verse in 4/4 and 3/4:

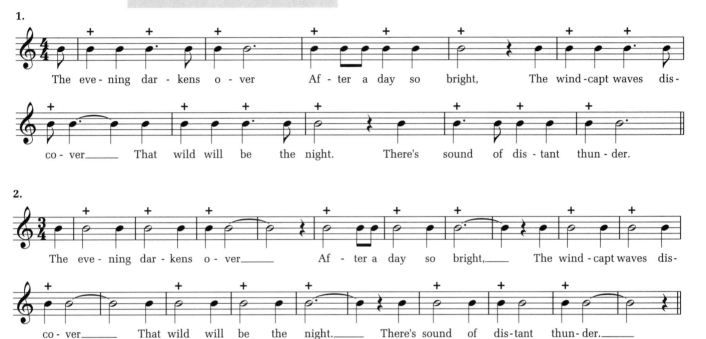

Providing the stressed syllables (shown as crosses in the examples above) are in the right place, you can adapt the words to fit any metre. Note that you will probably want to make some changes to this rhythm once you start setting the text to music, but it does provide a useful starting point.

To illustrate why understanding the stress patterns is important, compare the above rhythms with one that pays no attention to the natural stresses of the words. The sort of result below can happen if a melody is composed first and words are added at the last moment.

If you try saying the words to this rhythm it sounds very awkward. Unstressed syllables in the text are placed on strong beats of the bar and stressed syllables on weak beats, producing a very unnatural effect. Additionally, natural breaks in the text (such as between 'night' and 'there's') are ignored, weakening the meaning and structure of the text.

Now write a rhythm for your own text in a metre of your choice, aiming for the stressed syllables you underlined previously to occur on strong beats of the bar.

Step 5: deciding on the vocal style

There are broadly two types of setting to choose from. The first is to set the words to a melody in strophic form and then to devise an accompaniment. This would be appropriate if you wanted to compose in a lighter style for a vocal ensemble such as a close harmony group or a gospel choir, or just wanted to produce a simple setting for traditional choir. This type of setting is the more straightforward of the two approaches.

The second approach is to write a through-composed setting, where you respond musically to the text as you work through it. This would result in a different musical structure, built around the ideas expressed in the text. This is an approach more suited to a traditional choir as it tends to result in more complex music. It can be very satisfying finding ways to represent images in a musical way.

Decide which of these approaches you would like to take. If you choose the through-composed method, go straight to step 9. If you opt for the melody-and-accompaniment approach, go to step 6 but still read through the word-painting section in step 9, as you may be able to incorporate elements of word-painting into your setting.

> Both Edexcel and AQA Brief C candidates can choose to include an instrumental accompaniment. Common instruments and ensembles used to accompany choirs are solo piano, solo organ, solo harp, brass ensemble, string orchestra, chamber orchestra and symphony orchestra. If you choose to include instruments, think carefully about how and when you will use them: will they alternate with the choir, accompany the choir, double the choir, echo the choir or a mixture of all of these? Look at music scored for similar forces for ideas on ways to handle this sort of combination.

Step 6: devising a melody

If you have chosen a poem with, say, four lines to a verse, it should fall fairly easily into four-bar phrases. If your poem has a different number of lines, you may still be able to fit the text into this sort of phrase structure. Here is the first verse of *The Evening Darkens Over.*

> If you are following AQA Brief C, you can skip this step.

The first four lines fit a four-phrase melody well, but there is one line left over at the end. What is needed is some text to provide another three phrases of music, so that we can balance the first four-phrase melody with a second one.

Here is one solution:

The eve-ning dar-kens o-ver	Af-ter a day so bright,	The wind-capt waves dis-
co-ver____ That wild will be the night.__	Oh wild will be the night,____	
Wild will be the night.	There's sound of dis-tant thun-der,	Wild will be the night.

Here, the phrase, 'wild will be the night' has been repeated three times to form a sort of chorus that balances the opening four phrases of the melody. Repeating lines of text in this way is perfectly acceptable as long as you pick a suitable piece of text to repeat.

Compare the words in the melody above with the following: which do you prefer and why?

| 1. Wild will be the night,
Wild will be the night,
Wild will be the night.
There's sound of distant thunder. | 2. Wild will be the night,
There's sound of distant thunder.
Wild will be the night,
There's sound of distant thunder. | 3. There's sound of distant thunder,
There's sound of distant thunder,
There's sound of distant thunder,
There's sound of distant thunder. |

Now, on manuscript paper or at a computer, compose a melody for your own text, based on the rhythm you created in step 4, repeating words or phrases in your text as necessary to give your melody a strong phrase structure.

Step 7: devising an accompaniment

To create an accompaniment, it is first necessary to create a harmonisation of your melody, such as the one below for the first two phrases of *The Evening Darkens Over*.

Compose a harmonisation for your own melody. When you are happy with it, you can then devise a texture based around the notes of the chords for the remaining voices in whatever style you like. Treat the voices as melody instruments and do not worry about words at this stage. Here is a tango-style texture developed from the chords above:

> If you are an AQA Brief C candidate, you need to demonstrate an ability to use conventional chords and cadences in your harmonisation.

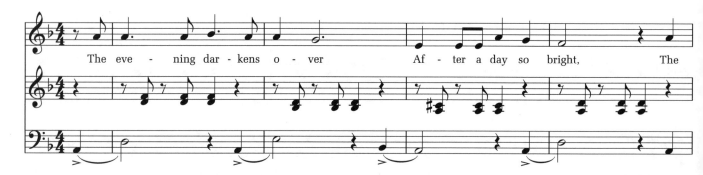

Notice that the middle parts move in a mostly stepwise way, and that the three accompaniment parts fit comfortably within the ranges of alto, tenor and bass respectively. Taking vocal considerations such as these into account at this stage will reduce the amount of rearranging you will have to do later.

If your text is in several verses, devise a different texture for each verse, going through the same process as before. Try to make each texture appropriate to the words being set (it might help you to read step 8 before working on these).

Here are some ideas for accompaniment textures:

➤ Sustained chords

➤ Shorter chords, perhaps on the off-beat

➤ Chords set to a repeated rhythm, perhaps involving syncopation

➤ Contrasting rhythms in the bass line and middle parts, as in the above example

➤ The melody moved to another part in the texture, for example the tenor

➤ An antiphonal texture

➤ A unison texture

➤ A homophonic texture

➤ Clapping, clicking fingers and stamping feet to add rhythm

➤ A melismatic solo vocal part above the melody and accompaniment, such as happens in gospel music.

On manuscript paper or using software, compose an accompaniment based on your harmonisation.

Text selection for the accompaniment

Once you have found a texture you are happy with, you will need to find words or sounds for the accompaniment to be sung to. Here are a few ideas:

➤ Select words from the text you are using

➤ Use onomatopoeic words, such as 'ding dong' for bells or 'miaow' for cats

> An onomatopoeic word is one that includes sounds like the noise to which the word refers.

➤ Use scat-like syllables, such as 'doo-be-doo', 'sha-boom' and 'doo-wop'

➤ Use wordless sounds, such as 'ah', 'ooh', 'mm' and 'ng'

➤ Use a mixture of the above.

For more rhythmic accompaniments, you will probably need some words with consonants in them, while more sustained accompaniments will work with 'ah', 'ooh' and 'mm' sounds. Lighter styles tend to use these types of syllable, while more 'serious', traditional styles tend to take the words from the text.

Remember that the choice of words in the accompaniment can affect how the setting comes across. For example, here are two possibilities for words based on the accompaniment above. How do they compare?

In the first example, the words in the melody are allowed to come across simply over the wordless accompaniment. In the second setting, the scat syllables of the accompaniment seem to mock the seriousness of the poem and sound rather out of place as a result. You would probably need a more lighthearted text and style of music for an accompaniment like this.

One thing to remember when devising vocal accompaniments is to make sure that the words do not obscure those in the top line: this is less of an issue if the melody is loud and the accompaniment quiet.

Now set suitable words to the different parts in your accompaniment.

Step 8: completing a strophic setting

To complete this type of setting, you need to compose the remaining verses. Refer back to your structure from step 2 and assess whether it needs changing now that you know how your first verse sounds. You will need to introduce contrast in the remaining verses. If you are using an ABA form, make sure that the B section contrasts in texture, key and mood. When you bring the A section back, try to adapt it to reflect the new words. If there are more than three verses, you could try treating the piece as a variation-form composition, concentrating on textural change: refer to project 1, steps 6, 10 and 11 for ideas of modifications you could make.

When you have finished, proceed to step 12 in this project.

Step 9: using word-painting

Word-painting is a valuable means of bringing the text of a poem to life. For example, words which suggests movement can be represented musically, through ascending and descending melodic lines to portray climbing or falling; through longer/shorter note values or slower/quicker tempi to suggest different speeds; and through crescendos and diminuendos for words like 'growing' and 'fading'. Other devices include changes of chord and key for words to do with change, and thinking up sounds or textures that imitate noises being described in the text, such as 'roar', 'chime', 'wind' and so on.

Here is a list of words from *The Evening Darkens Over* that could be illustrated musically, together with a suggested musical treatment of each:

Text	Musical setting
darkens	Move to a minor chord or lower register, or introduce chromaticism
bright	Move to a major chord or higher register
windcapt	Melisma to imitate wind
waves	Melody lines with wave-like contours
wild	Melisma, wide leaps
thunder	A low, booming bass line
hover/cliff/ height	A high soprano line against a low bass line
wander	A modulation, or a more rambling, melismatic melody
flutterings	Quicker notes, trills
as the sun goes under	Descending melody under a held pedal note
thick clouds	Low register, close spacings
rise	Ascending line
alone	A single note

A good next step would be to compose some ideas for each of these words. In the example below, ideas have been composed that all share the same tempo and metre ($\frac{4}{4}$). Although they do not always follow the rhythm created earlier, the stressed syllables are set to strong beats.

Read through your own text and write out any words or phrases that might be suitable for word-painting.

Text	Musical ideas

Now compose ideas to represent these images.

Step 10: extending your ideas

If you decided to jump from step 5 to step 9, the ideas you have produced so far will probably be quite short and may sound a little disjointed if played one after another. You will therefore need to find ways of developing and extending them, and of linking them to each other in a musically convincing way.

Let's look at the opening two ideas from *The Evening Darkens Over*. We have music for 'The evening darkens' and 'After a day so bright', so the only word missing is 'over'. The simplest solution for joining the two phrases would be to insert music for the word 'over' that links the two ideas together, like this:

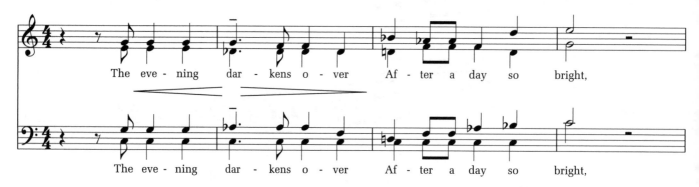

This seems to work well, but it happens a little too quickly for the words to make much impact. Perhaps 'evening' could be dwelt upon a little more so that 'darkens' has more of an effect, as in the next example.

Here, the original four-bar phrase has been extended to 11 bars. 'The evening' is repeated several times in an exchange between the women's and men's voices. To balance this, other words have been repeated as well. 'Darkens' is repeated in a falling sequence and 'after a day' is then repeated several times in a rising sequence that also involves imitation between the outer and inner parts.

There are, then, three different ways of repeating words illustrated here, which can be useful in making text last longer: repeating it between voices, repeating it in sequence and repeating it in counterpoint. Notice also how some of the original material – the rhythm of 'darkens', the harmonies of 'after a day' and the chord on 'bright' – has been modified so that the passage works better musically.

Develop one or two of your own ideas in a similar way, aiming to turn them into a more continuous section of music.

Overall, try to include a wide range of textures, but keep a logical strand running through the piece. Some textural ideas you might think about are unison, homophonic, contrapuntal, tune and accompaniment, antiphonal, using repeated notes, melisma, accents, staccato effects and exploring irregular rhythms and syncopation. Sudden loud or quiet passages and the dramatic use of silence can also be very effective.

> Listen to Britten's *Hymn to St Cecilia* for good examples of these.

To give your composition continuity, make sure that there is harmonic direction, that the melodies you use have a purposeful shape, and that the rhythms flow and sustain the momentum. Give each vocal part a coherent line that would make sense on its own. Keep listening to your piece from the beginning to check that it flows well and make amendments in places where it either becomes too dull or in passages which sound odd and out of place.

You can provide this by making sure that there is harmonic direction, that the melodies you use have a controlled shape, and that the rhythms flow and sustain the momentum. Try to give each vocal part a coherent line that would make sense on its own.

Step 11: completing a through-composed setting

You should by now have devised an overall structure and composed some melodic and accompanimental ideas. You now need to fill in the gaps, completing the music according to the structure you have devised.

Treat your text section by section, so if your piece uses an ABA form, approach section A first. Where you have already decided on particular musical effects or textures, try to plan in advance how you will fit these in. For example, if you have planned a high climax on the last word of a phrase, you know that on the words leading up to it the line will rise and get louder.

You are bound to find that the rhythms of the words do not always produce well-balanced musical phrases: sometimes you have too much text to fit in and at other times you will have too little. If you have too much, you may have to set the passage in another way. If you have too little, try repeating words and short phrases, if possible trying to use phrases that make sense on their own. You will almost certainly find yourself needing to change note values here and there.

Look for ways to bring back musical ideas later in your composition. A simple way of doing this is to set different words from near the end of the text to the same music as you had at the beginning. If this is practical, try to pick text that has a similar length and stress pattern. Even with text of a similar structure, you will probably need to change some rhythms to fit in the new words.

If you get stuck, go back to the text and think again of textural ideas that might work. Simple ideas are often the most effective: a unison passage, or a syllabic passage on a single chord might be the best way of proceeding.

Final steps

Step 12: ensuring your setting is practical

There are certain things singers find difficult, so if you can, try to make life as easy as possible for them by bearing in mind the following points:

1. Near the top of the range in all voices, it is harder to sing quietly and also more difficult for the words to be put across. At the very top of the range, try to use words with open vowel sounds like 'ah' and 'or' and avoid more 'closed' vowel sounds like 'i' and 'ee'. For example, 'star' and 'more' would be much more practical to sing in a very high register than 'thing' and 'sheep'.

2. Singers find awkward leaps difficult, as well as pitching notes out of nowhere. If this occurs, you may be able to swap notes around between parts or spell the notes differently, especially where a line goes from a sharp note to a flat note or vice versa.

3. Very high passages that last a long time can be very tiring, so try to avoid these if possible. Also, make sure your singers have somewhere to breathe in long, sustained passages.

4. If a word ends in a consonant, try to make sure that all the parts singing that note finish at the same time.

> If possible, try out your ideas on live singers. If you do not have enough, you could try multitracking one or two singers using an audio sequencer, if you have access to one.

Now go through the individual parts checking how easy they would be to sing.

Step 13: finishing touches

If you have not done so already, add performance details, including tempo markings, dynamics and articulation, making sure that all the markings are meaningful and consistent. Put dynamics above the music and lyrics below.

When writing syllables under notes, different syllables of the same word should be joined by hyphens. When working out how the syllables of a word should be divided, work out which letters in the word are actually pronounced at each point. In a melisma, a slur should be written over all the notes sung to the same syllable.

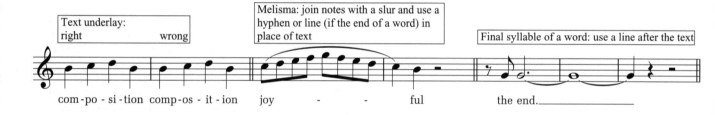

Project 3
Composing expressively: using a storyboard

This project is suitable for OCR Unit G352, Section B: Instrumental techniques or AQA Unit 2, Brief B: 2 Small Ensemble or 3 Electronic Music. It may also be used as the basis for Edexcel Unit 2 AOS1, Topic 1: Composing expressively, but you will need to devise your own storyboard to suit Edexcel's brief.

Introduction

Music is often used to illustrate a story or to accompanya visual art form, such as in film, television, musical theatre, dance or opera. Music in this context can be used to illustrate actions and events in the drama, to link or smooth scene changes, to create an appropriate mood and to suggest or enhance emotions. There are many ways of creating music that fulfils this purpose and this project will give you an opportunity to explore these in detail.

Suggested listening

There are ambush scenes in the following films:

- *Robin Hood Prince of Thieves* (composer: Kamen) – contains music for several short forest ambush scenes scored for orchestra.
- *The Kingdom of Heaven* (composer: H. Gregson-Williams) – a forest ambush scene takes place in the early stages of this film
- *Return of the Jedi* (composer: Williams) – contains battles between stormtroopers and rebels which take place in a forest, accompanied by orchestral music
- *The Terminator* (composer: B. Fiedel) – this may provide some ideas for a style of music that works well in an urban futuristic setting
- *The Lost World: Jurassic Park* (composer: Williams) – in the scene 'The Long Grass' the group of human survivors are attacked by raptors while crossing a field of long grass, accompanied by appropriate music
- *Planet of the Apes* (composer: Goldsmith) – the battle scene near the beginning of the film, where the human primitives are attacked by apes, is underscored by dramatic music in a dissonant musical style.

Step 1: choosing/devising a storyboard
The first questions you need to ask yourself are:

> Which medium am I writing for (film, TV, dance, opera, theatre (incidental music) or a concert (programme music))?

> What length will my composition be? (It will probably need to around three minutes, but check your exam board's specification.)

> Are there any specific guidelines given in the brief (for instance, depicting a shape of 'darkness into light')?

The answers to all of these questions are crucial to how you choose or design your storyboard. This, in turn, will ideally both inspire musical ideas and provide you with a structure. You can either devise your own, or adapt a scene from an existing film or play. In this project, the storyboard (detailed below) depicts an ambush. However, the steps we will be working through, and the advice given, can be applied just as well to a different storyboard, especially one in which two or more characters are in conflict.

Cue no.	Starts at...	What's happening on screen
1	0'00"	We see a group of weary travellers walking along a path in the open countryside, heading towards a forest.
2	0'21"	Cut to a group of robbers waiting in the woods. They hear the travellers approaching in the distance.
3	0'36"	Cut back to the travellers, who are making slow progress through the forest.
4	0'48"	Cut back to the robbers, who are getting ready to ambush the travellers. One steps on a twig.
5	0'57"	Cut back to the travellers, who, alerted by the noise of the twig, stop, terrified. They stay rooted to the spot, looking around them anxiously.
6	1'12"	The robbers suddenly jump out at them and a struggle ensues, with the travellers desperately fighting off the robbers.
7	2'12"	Eventually, the robbers run off into the woods, having stolen several of the travellers' possessions.
8	2'21"	The travellers sink in despair and reflect on their bad luck. Surely their plight could not get any worse.
	3'00"	End of scene.

Here, there are plenty of images at regular intervals to suggest musical ideas: the weary travellers, the threatening robbers, the anxious silence, the battle, the flight of the robbers and the despair of the travellers. There is also a clear structure to the scene, which will help give the music its own form: it begins and ends with the weariness of the travellers, and the intervening struggle with the robbers will allow two contrasted musical ideas to be pitted against each other as the two groups fight.

Think of the style of music you would like to write and adapt the details of the brief to suit. If you want to write for amplified instruments, you could change the setting to a present day one, moving it from the country to the city. If you would like to use synthesised sounds, you could transfer the story into the future or create a science-fiction setting. If you want to use world-music instruments, you could move the location to a foreign country. Moving the story back in time would enable you to use past musical styles, such as plainsong or medieval music.

This sort of brief is centred upon two contrasting forces, characters or points of view. It is a good idea to use one like this, as it will allow you to build a musical structure in which similarly contrasting ideas are played off against each other.

Composing the music

Step 2: mapping out the music

Start thinking of musical ideas that could illustrate the events of the storyboard well, and about how they will appear. At this stage it is enough just to describe the general features of the music, such as mood, tempo and suitable timbres.

In this particular brief, these might be as follows:

Cue no.	Musical material
1	Idea 1, travellers' theme: sighing music in a minor key played by strings
2	Idea 2, robbers' theme: rhythmic music, featuring drums, woodblocks, dissonant harmonies; quiet dynamic at this stage
3	Idea 1, but louder, with thicker texture
4	Idea 2 with more purpose, but still quiet
5	Idea 1, but using chords played very quietly, tremolando
6	Suddenly loud, with idea 2 being mostly used here, alternating with a more animated version of idea 1; incorporates changes of key and changes at a progressively faster tempo
7	Idea 2 fades out quickly, leaving idea 1
8	Idea 1 recapitulated, but slower moving, ending on a held chord that fades out

When writing music to accompany visual cues, timing is absolutely crucial, so you will need to calculate both the speed of the music and the number of beats it lasts for. Here is how the sections of the ambush scene could break down in terms of beats at different tempos:

	♩ = 60	♩ = 80	♩ = 90	♩ = 100	♩ = 120	♩ = 160
0'00"–0'21"	21	28	31.5	35	42	56
0'21"–0'36"	15	20	22.5	25	30	40
0'36"–0'48"	12	16	18	20	24	32
0'48"–0'57"	9	12	13.5	15	18	24
0'57"–1'12"	15	20	22.5	25	30	40
1'12"–2'12"	60	80	90	100	120	160
2'12"–2'21"	9	12	13.5	15	18	24
2'21"–3'00"	39	52	58.5	65	78	104

At ♩ = 80 tempo in 𝄴, all the cues would start at the beginning of a bar, so it would be simplest to pick this tempo or ♩ = 160. However, you can pick any tempo or metre you like – you can always make sections the right length through irregular metres, or by making the music slow down or speed up at certain points. As this is an imaginary brief, you can adjust timings later so that they fit your own composition better.

On manuscript paper, or using a sequencing or notation programme, map out the bars at the tempo and time signature you have chosen, and write down where the cues will start.

Step 3: deciding on instrumentation

Before choosing instrumentation, you will need to establish how you are going to write the music and how the performance of the music will be realised. Is the music for live performers? Will it be scored for synthesised and sampled instruments? Will it be developed through multitracking techniques in a studio? Or will it be a mixture of two or more of these?

My composition/performance methods will be:

....

....

....

Are there any instruments you would definitely like to include?

I will definitely include the following instruments:

....

....

You can now go about devising an ensemble, basing it around these instruments. Remember you can always change instruments or add more later. Aim for an ensemble whose instruments come from broadly the same musical tradition (unless the content of the story specifically suggests otherwise). You will probably need instruments to perform most of the following functions:

➢ Playing lyrical themes – for example, instruments such as oboe, flute, clarinet, violin, acoustic guitar, saxophone, wordless voice

➢ Playing more rhythmic, forceful themes – for example, instruments such as trumpet, trombone, saxophone, xylophone, lead guitar, square-wave synth sound

➢ Providing bass lines or sounds – for example, cello, double bass, tuba, bass guitar, synth bass

➢ Playing chords and accompaniments – for example, string orchestra, piano, organ, rhythm guitars, pad keyboard sounds

➢ Providing percussive sounds – for example, timpani, side drum, woodblock, tom toms, drum kit, synthesised drum kit, tabla (using pizzicato strings, or stab chords in brass/woodwind would also provide a percussive element)

➢ Adding richness and colour – for example, harp, glockenspiel, vibraphone, piano

➢ Sound effects – for example, rainstick, bell tree, guitar fret noise, birdsong. (Remember, though, that you will not be given credit for sound effects when your composition is marked.)

The full list of instruments in my ensemble is:

....

....

....

Step 4: creating musical ideas

You are now ready to start working on your musical ideas. Away from a musical instrument, visualise each cue in your head and the feelings of the people involved in it and then try to think of an appropriate musical idea. Describe this in words, for example 'slow, descending string melody accompanied by minor chords'. Whatever you think of in your head, be it the first notes of a melody, an idea texture or just a particular instrumental colour, will serve as a useful starting point.

Cue no.	Musical ideas

The first cue

Let's look at how we might approach the travellers' theme. Try to visualise as much about the scene as you can. What does the landscape look like? What is the weather like? How many travellers are there, and what is the make-up of the group? How well do they look? How fast are they moving? What are they carrying? What are they thinking?

Here is a possible idea to open this scene:

This solo phrase, with its slow tempo, descending shape and mournful sound of the oboe, could convey a sense of loneliness and despair. Does it have to be an oboe? Using software, compare this sound with  that of a recorder, a piano, a trumpet and an electric guitar. How do the different sounds affect the mood?

Here is an alternative opening idea:

This is a livelier idea that could work as an ostinato or riff. This use of a synthesiser implies a more contemporary setting for the story, the fast quavers adding a feeling of urgency and anxiety to the travellers' plight.

Here is an example of a less suitable idea, for piano:

This sounds far too happy and energetic for the scene. The major key and the lively accompaniment are more suitable for a fast-moving comedy scene.

Now devise your own idea for the opening scene. To check you are getting the right mood, play your idea to someone who does not know your storyboard and ask them to describe what sort of film scene it suggests to them.

Step 5: expanding your ideas

The next stage is to work out how to continue your idea. What happens in the scene? In the case of the ambush, do the travellers carry on walking in the same way, or do they have to stop and help each other? Are they walking from left to right as you look at them, towards you or away from you? Or are they moving more quickly, always on the lookout for danger? Such details as these will help you to work out how to pace your music.

To make the music fit into the correct time-span (in this case, 20 seconds), choose an appropriate tempo and work out how many beats this will fill. The tempo can be increased or decreased so that the section lasts a regular number of bars or beats.

If you are using Sibelius, the 'fit music to time' plug-in is very useful here.

Here is a possible continuation of the oboe idea:

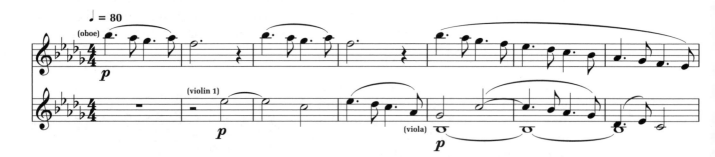

The oboe melody is repeated and extended downwards, while strings add sustained notes and a countermelody, underlining the despairing mood.

Here is a possible way of extending the synthesiser idea:

The two-bar phrase is used as an ostinato. Against it a syncopated second part is added, also using a synthesised sound. The high register and syncopation suggest a hesitancy and nervousness that might be appropriate for a group of people in unfamiliar surroundings.

Now extend your opening idea to fit the time-span of the cue and sustain the initial mood throughout.

Step 6: devising contrasting ideas

Cue 2 of our storyboard introduces a group of people who need to be portrayed as threatening, as a danger to the travellers. The music to accompany this cue should differ substantially from the travellers' music. Here is a possible opening for this section that would contrast effectively with the oboe and string music from earlier:

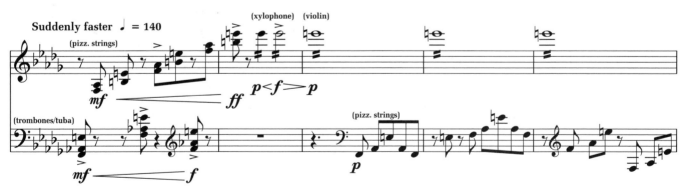

The complete change of tone colour that uses brass, pizzicato strings and xylophone, the sudden faster tempo, the dissonant harmony and the irregular rhythms help distinguish the robbers from the travellers. The furtive nature of the pizzicato figures and tremolo suggests that the robbers are waiting for something and the dissonance implies something sinister: this passage would not work as well if it was in a major key, without any chromaticism.

Although this passage looks complicated, it is all based on the notes of one chord. Rhythms, chords and melodic fragments have been built around the notes on the left.

Tip: A single chord can be an excellent starting point for generating material, as the notes of a chord can be turned into a melody, the chord can be given a rhythm and transposed.

Here is a possible contrast to the synthesiser music from earlier, again representing robbers:

This will contrast strongly with the first idea because it is in a bass register, there is a change of dynamic from piano to forte, a change of instrumentation to two distorted guitars and drum kit, and a new contrasting melody in a different key. All of these changes contribute to suggesting the separate identity of the two groups of people: if the second idea was also played on synthesisers, the contrast would not be so vivid. Notice, too how the distorted timbres of the guitars make the robbers seem threatening. Would this idea still sound threatening if played by bassoons or harp?

Now compose a contrasting idea to your previous one, to fit cue 2.

Step 7: adapting material to reflect developments in the storyboard

Now that you have particular material to represent each group of people, you can develop that material to reflect what that group of people is experiencing or feeling at different points in the story.

Here is how the oboe theme from earlier might change when the travellers enter the forest:

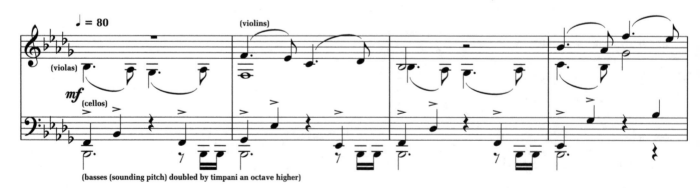

This music has been moved to a lower register and there is more going on, with a more insistently rhythmic accompaniment and imitation between the top two parts. The mood created here has a dark-toned quality because of the low register and key, while the accented rhythm in the cellos and basses suggests that walking is hard work.

The next cue for theme 1 is where the travellers hear a noise and freeze. A possible musical representation is shown below.

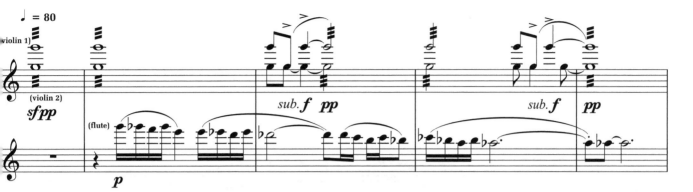

This time, the music is written in a very high register. The opening four notes of the melody have been speeded up and the pitch intervals between them reduced. The melody is now chromatic rather than diatonic and this, combined with the string tremolando and flute, creates an air of tension that fits the mood of the scene.

How much would the illustration of the storyline suffer at cue 3 and cue 5 if the music for cue 1 had been used unchanged at these points?

Now compose your own music for your cues 3, 4 and 5, developing your original ideas to reflect developments in the storyline. You might want to look back at steps 3–6 of project 1, for ideas on how to vary your material. Consider one or more of the following options:

➢ Slow down or speed up the idea

➢ Change it to a minor, major, chromatic or whole-tone idea

➢ Change the harmony

➢ Change the register or spacing

➢ Change the dynamic

➢ Change the texture

➢ Change the instrumentation.

Putting it all together

Step 8: making sections follow on from one another
In this project, there are frequent cuts between different musical ideas. The main difficulty with this type of structure is to ensure that the overall shape and flow of the music makes sense rather than coming across as a succession of unrelated sections.

How can you achieve this?
In places where the music passes backwards and forwards between ideas, make sure that there is a recognisable harmonic progression between the end of one section and the start of the next. This may involve transposing the new section.

The phrase structure is also important. In some sections you may want the new section to cut in unexpectedly, to highlight a surprise moment in the storyline. At other times, the music will hang together better if the new section happens at the natural end of a phrase.

As you compose more and more of your piece, you will need to listen to it carefully and decide whether the sections flow into each other.

Step 9: combining different material

Cue 6 of our storyboard describes the struggle between the travellers and the robbers, and so their music needs to be put together in some way at this point.

Combining ideas

In the following example, an idea developed from the travellers' theme has been put on top of the robbers' music, which serves as an accompaniment.

To combine two ideas like this, you will probably need to modify them. They will still be recognised if you keep the timbres of the original ideas and retain the basic melodic shape and the character of both ideas.

Here is one possibility for combining the two orchestral ideas:

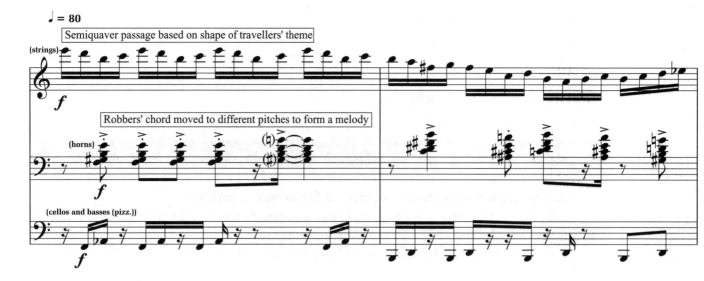

Here, the shape of the travellers' theme has been turned into a semiquaver passage, while the robbers' chord has been developed into a new theme by moving it around in parallel and giving it a syncopated rhythm. The cellos and double basses add further rhythmic excitement with a syncopated bass line.

Now try to combine your two themes in a similar way. Have them in different registers, one forming an accompaniment and the other a theme. Try to add rhythmic momentum through syncopation and cross-rhythms.

Rapid alternation of ideas

As the following ideas are so short, they can only contain a small amount of the original material. It is the contrast between the two ideas that matters, which in this case is to do with the register (high versus low) and timbre (synth versus guitars and drums). Notice that the alternation pattern is irregular and unpredictable, intensifying the drama.

Now compose a section that can be used in cue 6, in which you alternate rapidly between your two main ideas. The whole of cue 6 needs to maintain a strong sense of excitement. Here are some ideas of how to achieve this:

➢ Incorporate several changes of key and texture

➢ Change the instrumentation regularly

➢ Keep the rhythmic momentum going by not letting any rhythms become too repetitive; make use of syncopation and change accompaniment rhythms regularly

➢ Consider using loud, percussive instruments, such as snare drum, timpani, brass, or, if writing in a popular style, electric guitar, lead synth sounds and orchestra hits.

At the end of the robbery scene, you will need to depict the robbers overpowering the travellers and then running away (cue 7). This could be represented by a loud climax followed by the robbers' music fading out, disintegrating or ending in a descending or ascending scale.

Now complete the music for cues 6 and 7.

Step 10: bringing the composition to a close (cue 8)

Although this is a film-music composition, it is still important that it sounds like a self-contained whole, so the ending needs to round off the piece convincingly. The final section should be based on the travellers' music and will need to bring the music back to the mood of the opening. It would be a good idea to end in the same key as at the start, so you need to work out how to achieve this.

The opening of cue 8 could be a reprise of the opening with some sort of change to express the bleaker mood. Ideas to consider here are writing in a lower register, expanding or modifying the texture, filling out the harmony and slowing down the tempo. Consider gloomy musical colours such as a held, low pedal note, a slow, repeated drum stroke or a tolling bell.

Below is a possible ending for the extract scored for orchestra. Here, the tonic pedal and repeated timpani rhythm create a solemn mood, reinforced by the minor harmonies and the string-dominated scoring. The passage ends on a repeated held chord, which fades away.

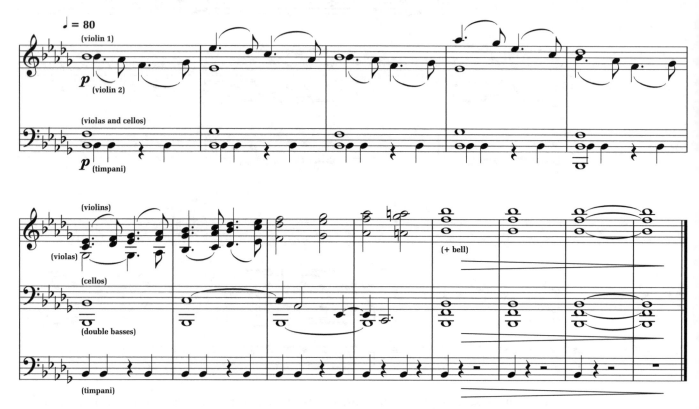

If your opening idea was faster-moving, a good way to transform its mood into something more gloomy is to double note values (for example, turning semiquavers into quavers). Here is a possible opening for cue 8 based on the synthesiser material from earlier:

Here, the repeated-quaver ostinato has been changed into downward arpeggios and the texture now covers a wide range. A melody has been added in the middle register and chord changes occur every two bars rather than every one. As with the orchestral music above, this passage also has a pedal, again suggesting a sense of finality. The passage could end with the arpeggios being further slowed down and coming to rest on a final chord.

Now compose your final section. Plan how many bars you will need and where the final chord should happen. Then construct a passage that leads the music from the preceding section to this final chord. Consider using rhythmic augmentation (lengthening note values) as you near the final note or chord.

Step 11: assessing the composition as a whole

Now that you have reached the end, listen carefully to the composition all the way through, following the storyline and assessing how effectively the music complements it.

Does the music:

➢ Capture the mood of each cue effectively?

➢ Distinguish between the robbers and the travellers effectively?

➢ Make sense as a whole?

If not, try to work out what you could do to improve it. With the second point, for instance, you could ensure that you always use a certain combination of instrumental sounds for the travellers and a different combination for the robbers (such as the synthesiser-versus-guitar sounds in the examples above). Do not be afraid to make radical changes if something is really not working.

Step 12: finishing touches

If you have not already done so, add dynamics, phrasing, articulation, tempo markings and other performance instructions.

Project 4
Writing for rock and pop instruments: verse-chorus form

This project is suitable for Edexcel Unit 2 AOS 2, topic 3 and AQA Unit 2, Brief B: 1 Vocal Music. It is also relevant to OCR Unit G352, Section B, arrangement of a lead sheet and AQA Unit 2, Brief C: Arranging. As some exam board briefs change from year to year, check with your teacher that this project fits in with your exam board's requirements.

Introduction

Verse-chorus form is the main form of pop and rock music. It is an ideal structure for a 3 to 5 minutes song, which is why it has proved so popular in commercial music. It is basically an extension of the form found in many folk songs and hymns, where a section comprising a verse and chorus is repeated for the duration of the song. Here the basic principle is that the music of both verse and chorus remains the same throughout, but words of the verse change with each repetition of the verse music, while those of the chorus do not.

Verse-chorus form was introduced as project 2 in the *GCSE Music Composition Workbook* (*Music Composition Workbook* Volume 1, Rhinegold 2008). This project will consolidate the technique of writing in the form and concentrate on stylistic and idiomatic writing, and on building up an integrated texture step by step. If you have the *GCSE MCW*, you are advised to read this through first to give you an overview of the form.

Standard verse-chorus *form*, which is explained in step 11, differs from this by including extra music at the beginning and end (the intro and outro), plus a contrasting section in the middle (the middle eight). However, in practice it is a very flexible form and many songs follow it only very loosely, for example changing the number and order of sections, inserting short linking passages called bridges and using more than one chorus.

Suggested listening
- Deep Purple: *Smoke on the Water* – the famous riff that introduces this song is more memorable than the verse and chorus material
- Linkin Park: *In the End* – this uses rap in the verse and singing in the chorus
- Lily Allen: *Smile* – both verse and chorus are based on the same repeated two-chord pattern
- Oasis: *Wonderwall* – instead of a middle eight, the chorus is repeated several times
- The Beatles: *Penny Lane* – the song is quite sophisticated harmonically and the chorus is in a different key from the verses

Preparation

Step 1: choosing a style
If you listen to a lot of pop and rock music, you will have a good idea of the many styles that exist, such as commercial pop music, emo, R&B, indie and techno.

When you write your song, you should try to make it stylistic. This doesn't mean that, if it is in a reggae style, it can only do things which can be found in reggae songs. You can combine different styles and influences (this is often what makes songs sound original), but you need to make sure that everything that is in the song should sound like it is meant to be there.

Choose a song or artist whose style you particularly like. Then list the reasons why the music sounds like it does: the instrumentation, the style of singing, the type of drum-writing, how sophisticated the harmony is and so on. This will be the starting point for your own song.

If you have a specific composition brief or a text you are required to set, some styles will be more appropriate than others.

Step 2: choosing an ensemble

Try to choose an ensemble that is in keeping with your chosen style. If you are writing for live musicians, you will also need to choose instruments played by people who will be able to perform or record your piece.

Here is a list of the most common rock instruments:

- Vocals. This could be male, female or male singing falsetto. Make sure you find out the range of the performer and their limitations.

- Backing vocals. If you are using studio techniques, you can overdub the same singer onto several different parts.

- Guitars. If you are writing for a guitar-based group, the normal guitar parts are lead guitar, rhythm guitar and bass guitar. If you are using studio techniques, you can record these with just one guitarist (provided that they play bass). Specify whether the guitars are acoustic or electric, and if there is any particular sound you would like (such as overdriven or distorted). Hawaiian guitars and banjos are also a possibility.

- Keyboards. Piano, electric piano, organ, synthesiser and samplers can all be used.

- Percussion. Drum. sets of different types (rock, synthesised, Latin, jazz, Indian, etc.) can be used. You can also add shakers, tambourines, cowbells, congas, timpani and so on.

- Other instruments. A string section, horn section or solo instruments such as trumpet, saxophone and flute could be added.

- Electronic, synthesised and sampled sounds. Many sequencers have software instruments emulating old instruments such as the mellotron, theremin and clavinet. You can also programme your own sounds using soft synths, such as the A1 on Cubase. A software sample is another possibility if you have access to one.

A basic ensemble will need a singer and a harmony instrument (guitar or keyboard), to which is often added a drum kit, bass instrument and melody instrument. You can also add any other instruments you need to fill out the texture, but be careful that they all fit within the same basic style and don't sound too disparate. You can also create fusion ensembles, where you combine the instruments of two different traditions, for instance rock instruments with Latin percussion.

Now choose a basic ensemble. If you are using a sequencer or studio techniques, you can always add other instruments later on if you require them.

My ensemble will include:

....

....

....

Step 3: lyrics

Writing your own lyrics has been covered in the *GCSE Music Composition Workbook*. Bear in mind that there is not credit for the quality of lyrics you write, only for the way you set them musically. You can either write lyrics before or after you compose the vocal part, but make sure that any lyrics you do write fit the mood of the music.

If the lyrics have been set for you, try to ensure that:

> The natural stresses of the words are reflected in the melody

> You set an appropriate mood for the text in each verse

> You spot any obvious opportunities for word-painting.

Refer to project 2 in this book for ways to put these points into practice.

Step 4: method of working

Decide how you are going to compose the song. You can follow any of the methods described on page 6.

If you are already used to composing your own songs, you will probably have found a method of working that you are comfortable with. Alternatively, your options may be limited by the facilities available to you. Whichever method you choose, make sure that you have a way of being able to improvise material, preferably against material you have already written.

Remember that you need to work alone: you are not able to submit group compositions.

Composing the verse

Step 5: composing a chord progression

Using chords from your chosen key, start with four chords which could be used to accompany a four-bar phrase, as in the example below. These could be used for the opening of the verse. Note that if you are writing for guitars, some keys are easier for them to play in than others. E, A, G and D are all good keys for guitars, in major or minor.

You could then repeat this progression, or perhaps change one or two of the chords. For a third phrase, you could either do the same thing again or, to make it more interesting, move away from the tonic. If this third phrase ends on a dominant chord, the music would then be prepared to go back to the tonic for the chorus. Here is how the first three four-bar chord progressions could look:

First two phrases start on tonic chord
Second phrase substitutes Am for the third chord

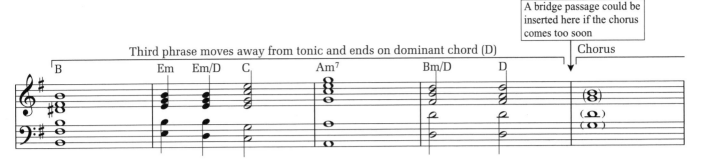

This chord progression mostly has one chord to a bar. However, the harmonic movement is free: you may find that in your particular style of music, you want more chords per bar, or fewer, or a different number from bar to bar.

For your chosen style of music, you might also find that this sort of chord progression is too rich. For instance, you may want to use only chords I, IV and V, or just use power chords for styles such as heavy metal, emo, punk, blues, heavy rock and reggae. On the other hand, you might find that more complex chords, such as 7th or 9th chords, are more appropriate to your style. Styles which use these sorts of harmonies include jazz, soul, music theatre, easy listening, funk and prog rock. Also consider using a chord progression in a minor key. Finally, remember that some songs do not use chords in the verse at all, perhaps just using a bass line and a drum track.

Now compose your chord progression. If you are setting words, you will need the number of phrases in the music to correspond with the number of lines of text in the verse.

Step 6: composing a melody over your chord sequence

The vocal lines in pop and rock music often have a very instinctive, natural quality, which mainly results from the fact that they have been worked out through improvisation. So, the best way to approach writing a melody in this project is to improvise it against the chord progression. You therefore need to find a way of being able to play the chord progression back and improvise over it. You could do this in any of the following ways:

➤ Play it on a harmony instrument such as a guitar or keyboard and improvise the melody by singing or playing against this

➤ Record the chord progression into a computer sequencer as an audio or MIDI track, play it back on a loop and record yourself singing or playing a live instrument as another audio track

➤ Record the progression as above, but use a MIDI keyboard to improvise, recording the MIDI data into the sequencer.

With these last two methods, you can record different takes and settle on one you like.

When improvising a melody, try to create ideas that are consistent with the style you are trying to create. Listen to songs in a similar style for inspiration. If you are using rapping techniques, the verse lyrics will be spoken, with chorus being sung, but you may still need some sort of instrumental melody, such as a bass riff, in the verse.

In Cubase, set the recording mode to 'stacked', set the locators either side of your chord progression and record in looped mode.

In Logic, set the cycle region, record in cycle mode and a folder of takes will be created automatically.

If you are writing your own lyrics, you will find that they either come at the same time as the melody, or that you only think about lyrics once you have composed the melody. However, don't worry about them too much, as the music is the most important thing at this stage. If you have already written the lyrics, try saying or singing them over the chord progression to find a rhythm that works.

Here are some possible melody openings for the first few bars of the chord progression above:

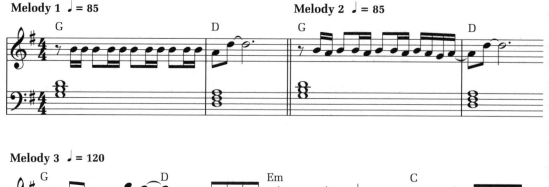

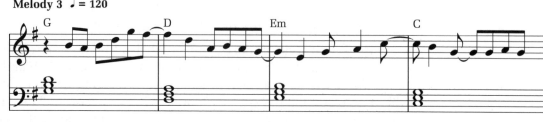

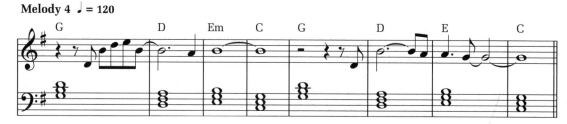

Melody 1 is a little dull as it is mostly on the same note and the rhythm is fairly square.

Melody 2 is a more developed version of melody 1. It has more interest as it alternates between two notes in the first two bars and incorporates some syncopation, giving it more of a natural feel.

Melody 3 has a wide range and a more varied contour, being based on the notes of the accompanying chords, and would require a good singer. Notice again the use of syncopated rhythms, which help the line to flow.

Melody 4 is a more lyrical melody, using sustained notes that will allow the vocalist or instrumentalist to be expressive. Writing a slow melody like this is well worth considering, and might form a good contrast with a faster-moving line elsewhere in the song. Notice that the second four-bar phrase repeats the harmonies of the first four bars, a change to the original chord progression. You might find that you need to change the chord progression if your melody takes you in a different direction.

When you feel you have found the right opening, you can extend it for the duration of the complete chord progression. Aim to keep the same character, perhaps by starting each phrase with the same rhythm or melodic outline, but also try to give the line some overall shape, such as getting gradually higher, including increasingly large intervals or covering an increasingly wide range of notes. Here is how a continuation of melody 2 might look:

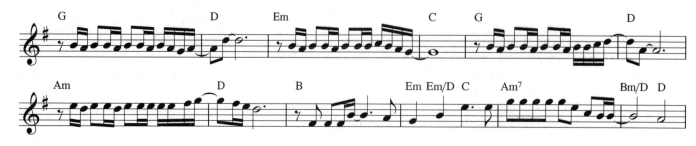

Now compose a melody for your chord progression. Bear in mind the limits and range of the performer you are writing for. Give the melody a strong shape, with phrases which fit in with those of the chord progression.

Step 7: creating a drum pattern

When you begin adding a drum pattern to your melody and chord progression, the overall mood and feel will begin to take shape. If you are not intending to include a drum track (for instance, if your composition is for voice and guitar only), you will need to add a rhythmic element to your accompaniment instead. This is covered in step 8.

A good first step is to start with a simple drum pattern of one, two or four bars. If you are using a sequencer, you can build up a drum track one instrument at a time, setting the software to record on a loop in mixed mode and then overdubbing the instruments one by one. You can then cut and paste this loop to form a continuous track.

Although you are advised not to use commercial drum loops, if you have access to any, you could look at some of these for ideas and then base your own ideas on them. The 'add drum pattern' plug-in on Sibelius might be a good place to start, although of course you can't use these in your piece. Alternatively, listen to the drum tracks on actual songs.

Concentrate first on the bass drum, snare and hi-hat. At this stage, you are looking for something that will give you the right feel, so you can add details later. Here are some patterns to try out with your existing material:

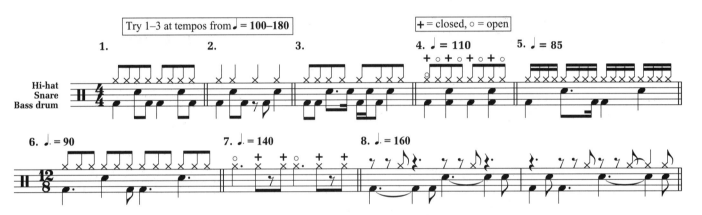

The first five are straight rhythms in 4/4 while numbers 6–8 are swung and written out in 12/8. Note that you can also use less common metres, such as 3/4 or 5/4.

Once you have a basic pattern, this should provide you with a good starting point. Although it is tempting just to repeat this pattern all the way through your song, doing this can make your song sound rather repetitive. Your song will be more effective if you vary the drum pattern intelligently.

In the last bar of a four- or eight-bar phrase, the drums often play a **fill** – a mini solo, where they depart from the basic pattern. When leading into new sections, the fill is often quite prominent and inventive. It usually involves more of the instruments in the kit, especially toms, and can end with a crash cymbal on the barline.

Here are some examples:

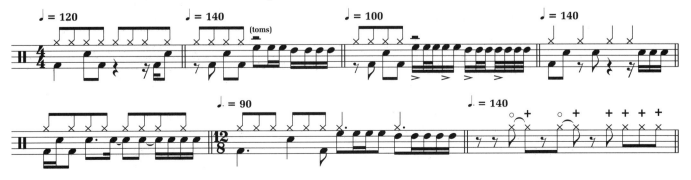

In new sections (such as the beginning of the bridge or chorus), the basic pattern might be changed slightly, for instance by changing one of the sounds, or by adding an extra one. It is common for drum parts to be thinner at the opening of the verse and gradually to get more complex as the chorus approaches.

Here is an example of how drum pattern 3 might develop across a verse, incorporating fills and changes to the drum pattern:

Think about incorporating some of the following other sounds, especially at new sections:

➤ Cowbell

➤ Agogô

➤ Woodblock

➤ Tambourine

➤ Maracas

➤ Ride cymbal hit on the bell or the rim

➤ Rim shot on snare drum

➤ Playing with brushes instead of sticks (common in jazz).

If possible, get a drummer to demonstrate some standard patterns and fills to you and to try out patterns you have written. There will be limitations to what a live drummer can play, so if you are writing for one, make sure that they do not have to play more instruments simultaneously than they can physically manage with their hands and feet.

Now complete your drum track for the verse.

Step 8: accompaniment rhythms and bass lines

You should by now have the raw ingredients for a verse – a melody, some chords and a drum track. To give your song character, the next step is to make your accompaniment more interesting.

As with the drum part, first develop an accompaniment pattern of one or two bars that complements the other parts and sets the desired feel. Here are some possible starting points:

The first six of these ideas are based on chords, the last three on broken chords. Note that these are all for guitar but could also be played on a keyboard. Try these patterns out with your own chords and see how well they work. You will probably have to adjust their rhythm so that they fit with your particular melody and drum track.

If you can't find something you're happy with, come back to the accompaniment rhythm once you have composed a bass line.

As with the drum part, a repeated rhythm in the accompaniment can get predictable. You might need to vary it, for example by changing the pattern slightly at a new phrase, or using a two- or four-bar rather than a one-bar pattern. Remember that, if you are writing for guitar, what you write needs to be playable on guitar. Try it out on a guitarist if you can, especially if you are writing chords.

For more keyboard patterns, see project 5.

Now compose your own accompaniment pattern. Note that in some cases, you might not need to do much to the rhythm of the chords at all, as it might make the texture too cluttered.

Step 9: bass line

The bass line is important in giving your song direction and purpose. If you are writing for a separate bass instrument, such as an electric bass guitar or acoustic bass, this will give you the freedom to compose an independent, purposeful bass line. If your bass line is being incorporated into a guitar or piano part that is also providing the harmony, still try to ensure that it has shape.

It is common for the bass line to play the bottom note of the chord whenever there is a chord change. For the rest of the duration of the chord, the bass tends to either repeat or sustain the bass note, or play a melodic line based on the notes of the chord. A good bass line can make the whole texture sound more exciting through syncopation and upbeat rhythms.

Here are five different bass lines that could be written around the same progression:

Now compose your own bass line, making sure it fits in with both your melody and your drum part.

Step 10: putting the complete texture together

You can now put the melody, accompanying chords, drum part and bass line together to form a complete texture for the verse. You may find that it doesn't all work straight away. You might have to adjust some of the parts in the texture if there is too much going on. One thing you could consider is to build up to the full texture bit by bit. For instance, the verse could open with just the melody and chords, and then the bass line and drum part could be added later.

The complete texture for the worked example is on the opposite page:

Note that the ideas from earlier have been rewritten in double note values to make it easier to read. The chords in the lead guitar have been rewritten as power chords, with the third omitted, creating a rawer sound at these points. The bass line both adds rhythmic impetus and offers melodic interest, providing movement when the melody is still. The drum part mostly follows the same four-bar pattern, but changes after the fourth phrase of the melody. Notice how the texture changes in the fifth phrase of the melody, with held chords in the guitar instead of repeated ones. The slight change of mood here could be reinforced by introducing other instruments, such as a string section doubling the chords at a higher octave, or a lead guitar adding a countermelody.

Now complete the full texture for your verse, aiming to keep it interesting by introducing subtle changes in the texture where necessary.

Completing your song

Step 11: composing the other sections

You should now have been through the process of composing material for a verse, from a simple chord progression through to a final texture. You can compose all the other sections in your piece in the same way, following the verse-chorus structure.

Project 2 in the *GCSE Music Composition Workbook* covers the parts of the verse-chorus form in detail, so only a summary of the typical features of each section is given.

Introduction	Features that will appear later in the song often appear here. The introduction often has a thinner texture than the main part of the song, for instance often consisting of just the bass line, chord progression or a melodic hook.
Verse 1	This is the material you have written so far. In the lyrics, the verse is the part where the words are different each time.
Bridge	This is a short passage which links the verse to the chorus. You might need to write a bridge if you find that the verse ends in the wrong key, or if the chorus needs more preparation to give it an impact. A bridge could be based on a chord progression which works its way back to the home key, or it might be a way of drawing out the final chord of the verse. It usually has a slightly different texture to the verse.
Chorus	This should contrast with the verse. In the lyrics, the chorus is the section of text which is repeated and often contains the title of the song. Normally, the chorus has a simpler melody that could be sung along to, but also a fuller texture. Often the harmony is thicker, with backing vocals and strings perhaps doubling the melody in 3rds or 6ths. Textures tend in general to be more sustained.
Verse 2	Change something to make verse 2 different from verse 1. For example, change the timbre of one of the instruments, or, if you are using audio sequencing software, use different effects.
(Bridge)	
Chorus 2	This is a repeat of chorus 1. As with the verses, it can be changed slightly.
Middle eight	The vocals often drop out here, being replaced by a solo instrument playing a melodic improvisation. New material is often introduced, such as a different chord progression, though it is still consistent with the style and material in the rest of the song.
Chorus 3	This can be a straight repeat of the opening choruses, but it might be more interesting to vary some of the material here. This could involve adding another part on top of the existing texture, such as a solo for trumpet, vocals or lead guitar.
Chorus 4	Further repeat of the chorus. This may contain further improvisation or different added parts, and may fade out or come to rest on a cadence
Outro	This section brings the song to an end, perhaps bringing the song to a cadence. A lot of songs just fade out with the chorus repeating. It might mirror the way the song opened by returning to the texture, tempo or material of the introduction.

Step 12: finishing touches

When you have composed a complete song, listen to it carefully and check that it holds together. In particular, listen for strong textural contrast between the verse and the chorus, and identify any places where the song loses momentum, or becomes too repetitive. You can overcome this by introducing textural or rhythmic changes at these points.

When preparing either a live or synthesised recording to be mixed down, make sure that the instruments are all panned appropriately. Ensure that each instrument can be heard clearly in the texture. This can be done by adjusting panning and volume, and altering the EQ. You may want to add some effects on one or more tracks, such as some reverb on the voice. If you do this, make sure that all the tracks can still be heard clearly, as it is easy to get carried away.

Make scores as clear and informative as you can. They should have a tempo marking, dynamics, phrasing and articulation. You may have problems with the score if exporting it as a MIDI file from a sequencer. If this is the case, you might need to produce a separate MIDI file of your song in your sequencer, in which you quantise all the data and then export it as MIDI data.

Project 5
Piano and keyboard writing: a rondo

This project is suitable for AQA Unit 2, Brief B 4 Keyboard Music. Depending on the specified brief, it may also be suitable for Edexcel Unit 2 Area of Study 1, Topic 1 or 2. As some exam boards' briefs change from year to year, you should check with your teacher that this is an appropriate project to follow. The advice on keyboard writing is applicable to any composition using a keyboard instrument.

Introduction

Piano and keyboard writing

Keyboard instruments have been central to music of many cultures. At any given time since the 16th century, one or more of the harpsichord, organ and piano have been prominent in classical music, and the piano, Hammond organ and numerous types of electronic keyboard have found their way into popular music. The advantage of keyboard instruments is that they can play many notes or parts at the same time, meaning that a solo performer can play a solo or accompaniment that would take several non-keyboard players to perform otherwise. Furthermore, keyboard instruments have always been very popular with composers as they provide the opportunity to try out and hear quite complex ideas.

> **Suggested listening**
> - Couperin: *Les Moissonneurs* – an example of a rondo in a baroque style, written for harpsichord, using mostly contrapuntal textures
> - Mozart: *Rondo Alla Turca* (from Sonata in A major K. 331) – a very well-known rondo, composed in a classical style
> - Chopin: Rondo in E♭ major, Op.16 – a virtuoso large-scale rondo in a romantic style. The individual sections are comparatively long and the piece also contains a long introduction
> - Ravel: Pavane pour une infante défunte – a rondo in a fairly slow tempo in a very melodic style, using a rich harmonic language
> - Bartók: No.1 of 3 Rondos über Volksweisen (piano) – the rondo theme is based on a simple folk tune, while the episodes are faster and more rhythmic, using a more adventurous harmonic language
> - Dave Brubeck: *Blue Rondo à la Turk* – a jazz rondo. Short extracts from the fast, irregular metre rondo theme, which opens and closes the piece are used to interrupt the long, central, walking bass solo section.)

Rondo form

What is a rondo? A rondo is a musical form where a rondo theme returns regularly throughout a piece, interrupted by contrasting material that makes up episodes. If the theme is represented by the letter A, the form might be ABACA, ABACABA or ABACADA, where B, C and D represent the different episodes. It is a good way of creating a structure which has both unity and contrast, which will allow you to explore a number of keyboard techniques.

It is a good idea to use a tonal scheme in which you explore related keys in the middle three sections, such as tonic minor, dominant and relative minor. The final A section should be in the tonic. The rondo in this project is in ABACA form.

Preparation

Step 1: choosing your instrument(s)

The instrument(s) you choose will in part be determined by the requirements of your exam board's specification, so you are advised to check this thoroughly.

Writing for a solo keyboard instrument or tuned percussion instrument is the most straightforward option. Solo piano is the most obvious choice here, but also consider organ, electronic keyboard, harpsichord, celesta, marimba, vibraphone and xylophone. Bear in mind that the last five have their own limitations, such as a smaller range (celesta), a limited dynamic range (harpsichord) or a maximum number of notes playable at the same time (xylophone).

Combining two or more keyboard players is another option. The most common combinations are:

> ➤ Piano four hands (two pianists at one piano)

> ➤ Two-piano duet (two pianists and two pianos)

> ➤ Keyboard ensemble (two or more keyboards)

> ➤ Percussion ensemble (for instance xylophone and vibraphone)

> ➤ Piano and percussion ensemble.

Jazz ensembles sometimes use a Hammond organ or vibraphone in place of the piano.

This last type of ensemble would allow you to write thicker and more varied textures, but it can be more complicated to get the performers together. Highly rhythmic pieces and minimalist ideas tend to work well with this sort of ensemble.

A third possibility is to combine a keyboard instrument with instruments from other families. Typical ensembles of this kind include piano quartet (piano, violin, viola and cello), and jazz chamber ensemble (piano, bass, drums and a choice of trumpet, clarinet, saxophone, trombone or violin).

When choosing your ensemble, check that the right performers are available and that the instruments can be brought together: there is no point writing a piece for two pianos if you cannot get the instruments together in the same room.

Now choose your ensemble. If possible, try to listen to some music written for that combination to hear the sorts of sounds it can produce.

Step 2: deciding on the musical style of the composition

Although this project is in rondo form, it need not dictate the style of your composition. You can select any style as long as it conforms to your exam board's requirements. Possibilities include most classical styles (Classical, Romantic, Impressionist, 20th-century), jazz, blues and Latin. For electronic keyboard ensembles, ambient electronica is a possibility. The styles covered in this project are classical, jazz and Latin.

Make sure your style and ensemble suit each other. You can always change the ensemble to suit your chosen style, rather than the other way round. Once you have chosen your style, try to listen to some recordings of music in that style to give you some ideas.

Composing your piece

Step 3: composing and harmonising a rondo theme

Aim to make your rondo theme catchy and memorable so that when it returns later in the piece, the listener will be able to recognise it instantly. It should also sound complete, ending with a cadence in the key in which it started. Many successful rondo themes are in a fairly quick tempo and not too serious in tone. A conventional 16- or 32-bar theme in four-bar phrases would work satisfactorily (see project 1, step 1 for advice on composing a theme), but feel free to try something else if you wish. For a three-minute piece, a rondo theme of about 30 seconds would be about the right length.

On manuscript paper or at a computer, compose your theme, then harmonise it using simple triads.

Step 4: devising an idiomatic texture for your theme

It is important that your theme is suitable for the keyboard instrument for which you are writing. Try to develop your simple chordal harmonisation into a texture that works well on your instrument. Piano examples are explored below, but you will need to bear the following in mind if you write for other keyboard instruments.

With a **pipe organ,** there is no sustaining pedal, but notes last as long as they are held down. Most instruments have a pedal board on which the feet can play simple bass lines and pedal notes. There are often two or more manuals (keyboards), so you can use several different sounds at the same time using the organ's stops, which set the keyboards to control different rows of pipes. As organs differ so much, it is essential to consult an organist and try out your ideas on an actual organ. Keyboards are not velocity sensitive, but there is some control over dynamics through the use of a 'swell pedal'.

Harpsichords have a range of five octaves and notes are played at the same dynamic regardless of how hard the keys are struck, so complicated textures can sound rather muddy. There is no sustaining pedal.

The **celesta** has a range of five octaves and sounds one octave higher than written. It has no sustaining pedal, is very quiet and its notes fade quickly.

Synthesisers, like organs, often have a wide range of possible sounds and **MIDI keyboards** can also be used to trigger samples or computer software. Depending on the keyboard, there may also be a sustaining pedal, pitch bend and modulation wheels which can be exploited. Most keyboards are velocity sensitive, so you can include detailed dynamics.

Tuned percussion instruments (such as **xylophone**, **glockenspiel**, **marimba** and **vibraphone**) are played with beaters, normally a maximum of two in each hand. This means that the maximum number of notes in a chord is usually four, so you will need to 'spread' chords if you want more notes. It is best to keep to one or two part writing for most of the time. Remember that xylophone and marimba notes fade very quickly so to sustain notes, tremolandos are often used. Vibraphones have a sustaining pedal and can produce a vibrato effect if their motor is turned on. Ranges of tuned percussion instruments often vary, so check on an actual instrument. The glockenspiel sounds two octaves higher than written and the xylophone one octave higher.

Below are several ideas for classical piano textures that are all derived from the same melody and chord progression. If possible, try these out or listen to someone else playing them and then develop your own texture, based on your theme and chords, in the same way.

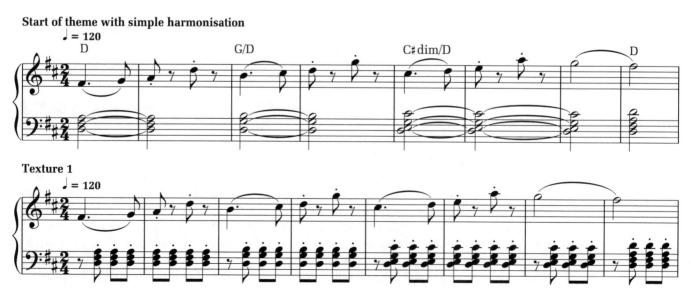

Texture 1 uses repeated chords, but notice that there is often a rest on the first quaver. This gives the accompaniment a light feel.

In **texture 2**, the left hand has a tonic pedal, which is once again given a springy, lively feel by the frequent rests on the main beats of the bar. The harmony is moved into the right hand, with a second part added to the melody.

Texture 3 is more sustained, with the left hand playing arpeggios that span two octaves. The sustaining pedal would need to be used here.

In **texture 4**, the harmony is again moved into the right hand, while the left hand has rapid semiquaver figuration based on a turn.

Texture 5 is more Romantic. Here, the theme has been moved down to the left hand, while the right hand has triplet arpeggios spanning two octaves. Again, this would require the use of the sustaining pedal.

These ideas are in a classical piano style, but you might prefer to write in a different idiom. Here is an idea in a more jazzy style that could be developed into a number of different popular styles:

The theme as it stands conveys a jazzy mood, but the semibreve rhythm in the accompaniment is rather unimaginative and needs to be developed. Notice that the harmony uses 7th chords. These are very common in jazz and, generally speaking, you should try to include plenty of both these and 9th chords if you want to harmonise a melody in a jazz style.

In **texture 6**, the same G^7 chords have been slightly respaced and shared between the hands to make them playable. The chords are played as syncopated stabs, which keeps a strong sense of rhythm without cluttering the texture. Notice how the music has been rewritten in triplets so that the swung rhythm can be accurately notated.

In **texture 7**, similar syncopated chords have been moved into the right hand, which also has the tune. The left hand walking bass line in broken octaves is a very common feature of jazz, blues and boogie-woogie. It is idiomatic (though tiring!) for jazz pianists and is a good way of adding rhythm to a bass line.

Texture 8 is in a bossa nova style. The theme is now in the major and the chords have been rewritten as major 7th chords so as to be more in keeping with the style. The right hand has the melody as well as the upper notes of the harmony, while the left hand just plays the bass line.

There are a few general points to make about piano accompaniment textures:

➢ Always try out your piano music on a real piano, or ask someone else to. This is both to check that it is playable and because real pianos sound very different from software-based or digital pianos.

➢ With a melody-and-accompaniment texture, you will often have to share the inner parts of the chords between the hands, particularly if there is a moving bass line.

➢ When writing close-position chords (where the notes are as close to each other as possible), try not to write any more than four notes per hand, and keep the spread of chords to not more than an octave.

➢ When writing open-position chords (where the notes are more widely spread), do not write more than three notes per hand, and limit the spread to a 10th at most.

➢ If a chord is not playable, try respacing it or removing notes from it which already appear in a different octave.

➢ Try not to have thick harmonies low down they keyboard, as these will sound muddy. Respace chords in open position if they sound too dense.

➢ To keep a texture moving, make sure that there are plenty of rests in it: think about removing accompaniment notes which fall on the strong beats of the bar, or which coincide with notes in the melody. Shortening notes in the melody may also help.

Now compose your rondo theme and accompaniment in an appropriate style. Remember that it should have a clear ending and should finish in the key in which it started.

Step 5: composing your episode 1 material

The episodes of a rondo are designed to contrast with the rondo theme, so it is a good idea to introduce a new idea with a different texture. If writing in a classical style, this could be some sort of passagework, or a contrasting melody and accompaniment.

Here are some ideas which could be used to contrast with the theme from earlier:

Circle of 5ths chord progression

These ideas are more technically demanding for the player than the opening ideas for the rondo theme. Notice that the chord progression is in the tonic minor (D minor) as opposed to the major key of the theme. This is a simple way of giving the episode a different character. This particular sequential chord progression, where the chord pattern repeats every two bars on a different degree of the scale, means that whatever you do in bars 1–2 will also work in bars 3–4, 5–6 and 7–8 (although you may need to adjust individual notes to fit the key that you are in). So, once you have set up a texture for the first two bars, the next six are much easier to complete.

Texture 9 is in two parts which each alternate a bar of scalic material with a bar of harmony or broken chords. The two parts appear to echo each other, but with their scales going in opposite directions. This type of texture, where the two parts swap material at regular intervals, can be quite dramatic and is a useful device to remember. Writing scales based on a chord progression is not as hard as you might think. Begin the scale on a harmony note, stick to notes from the scale of the key the music is in at the time, and end on the harmony note of the new chord when the change of chord is reached. You can insert chromatic notes or miss notes out to enable you to end on the note you want.

Texture 10 is quieter and more lyrical. It could be used as an effective contrast with a loud, showy rondo theme.

Texture 11 shows a quite common but very effective piano technique, where notes are played alternately in each hand at a fast speed. This is a good way of making a fairly simple passage (for instance both hands doubling each other in octaves) more exciting.

Note that although this passage is in contrary motion, it would work just as well in parallel motion.

Texture 12 has a repeated syncopated rhythm in the right hand and off-beat quavers in the left hand, which fill in the right hand's rests. You can invent a similar texture by creating a rhythm that lasts for the duration of a chord and repeating it at every chord change.

Texture 13 has broken octaves in the left hand (similar to texture 7) and chords in strong dotted rhythms in the right hand. The bass line links the lowest note of each chord with a scale. Notice how chromatic notes are used to ensure that the bass line arrives on the right bass note at the beginning of each bar. Repeated chords have a lot of impact on the piano, especially when in dotted rhythms.

If you can, try out these textures or ask someone else to. Compose a texture of your own based on the above chord progression.

Then compose your own chord progression, perhaps starting in the tonic minor, and modulating to a related key by the end, and create your own piano texture in a similar way. Remember that it should contrast in mood with the rondo theme. To give the episode some shape, construct the chord progression in regular phrases, for example of four or eight bars in length. If your rondo theme is 30 seconds long, the overall length of the episode could be about 40 seconds.

For a jazz-style composition, the episode could be more of a melodic improvisation, perhaps using a repeated chord progression. This could be taken from the chord progression of the theme or you might devise a new one, perhaps based on the blues scale. If you are writing for a jazz ensemble, the solo could be taken by one of the other instrumentalists.

Alternatively, the episode could be more of a harmonic development, exploring more sophisticated harmonies and chord progressions.

Jazz episode
Here is an idea of how you could go about creating material for a jazz episode:

1. Compose a chord progression that uses standard chords.

Chord progression

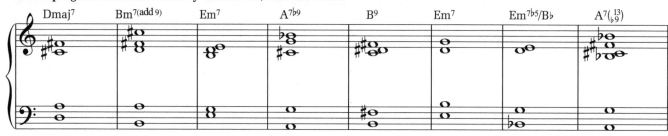

Chord progression made richer by added 7ths, 9ths and 13ths

Texture 14: building a melody around the notes of the chords

Texture 15: adding a melody over the chord progression

2. Enrich the chords by adding major or minor 7ths, major or minor 9ths, or other intervals.

3. Once you have a chord progression you are happy with, you can go about constructing a melody-and-accompaniment texture around the notes of the individual chords. Try to establish a rhythmic flow by using frequent syncopations and by not making the rhythm too repetitive.

4. You could further develop the material by writing melodic lines that link different notes in a chord through stepwise movement, and adding chromatic notes. Again, keep the rhythm moving by using syncopation in either the melody and the accompaniment or both.

5. Now complete your jazz episode.

Step 6: the return of the rondo theme

When the rondo theme returns for the first time, the main priority is that it should be instantly recognisable. If you have modulated to a related key, you will need to transpose the rondo theme to the new key, although you can keep the melody and texture the same as the original. However, you can make other small changes, to add a little interest. These could be:

➢ Changing the key from major to minor, or vice versa

➢ Writing the theme in a different register (such as high up)

➢ Presenting the theme at a different dynamic

➢ Changing the instrumentation (if your piece is for an ensemble).

If you decide to make changes, try to ensure that this passage provides an effective contrast to episode 1.

Step 7: composing episode 2

Episode 2 will need to do two things. First, it should contrast with both the rondo theme and with episode 1. Second, it needs to modulate back to the tonic for the final return of the rondo theme. As with episode 1, it should last roughly 40 seconds.

You could compose this episode in a similar way to episode 1, by devising a chord progression and then composing a texture and perhaps a melody around it. Look again at the textures under step 5 and think about modelling your episode on one of these.

If composing in a jazz style, you could again write a more improvisational section here. Try to make it contrast in mood with the improvisation in episode 1. You could change the register, and make the solo more showy (using fast runs and arpeggios), more fragmentary (breaking it down into isolated syncopated notes) or more melodic, composing a lyrical solo. If you are composing for a jazz ensemble, think about giving the solo to an instrument whose sound and register contrasts with those of the solo instrument from the first episode. Having a trumpet and a bass as the two solo instruments, for instance, would be a good contrast.

Step 8: final statement of rondo theme

The most important thing here is that the theme should be in the tonic, so if it is not, you will need to rewrite the end of episode 2 so that the music modulates back to the tonic key. The final statement of the rondo theme can be the same as the first, but try to make the ending sound final. You could do this by repeating the rondo theme, or the final phrase of it, at a loud dynamic, perhaps using a thicker texture. A tonic pedal can be an effective device to use at this point.

If your ending does not sound final enough, you might need to add a short coda that ends with a cadence in the tonic key. You might also think about a 'joke' ending, where the music tails off or stops unexpectedly and is then rounded off with a sudden loud cadential progression. Another way to end the piece might be to slow down and end on a held final chord.

If you are writing in a jazz style, a common ending is for the final chord to be enriched by piling more and more added notes onto it (for instance by going up in 4ths). The final chord might also be played tremolando, or have a free improvisation over the top of it, often ending in a glissando to a low note and a sudden cut-off.

Now write out the final statement of the rondo theme and compose an effective ending.

Step 9: finishing touches

Once you have reached the end of your rondo, assess how it works as a whole. Do the episodes contrast effectively with the rondo theme? Does the piece contain tonal variety? Does it work well as a whole: are the lengths of the different sections well balanced? Is the piece playable? Make any amendments you think are necessary.

Finally, if you have not already done so, add dynamics, phrasing, articulation, tempo marks and indications for pedalling, ensuring that any markings you do put in make sense practically and musically.

Glossary

Alberti bass. A simple accompaniment pattern based on broken chords. The notes of each chord are played in the following order: lowest, highest, middle, highest. Popular in 18th-century keyboard music, it was named after the composer Domenico Alberti who was particularly attached to the device.

Antiphonal. Adjective to describe a texture that uses antiphony, which is the musical alternation of two or more groups of spatially separated performers.

Appoggiatura. An ornamental note that falls on the beat as a dissonance and then resolves by step onto the main note.

Articulation. The extent to which a series of notes are detached from or connected to each other. Directions such as staccato, legato, tenuto and sforzando change the articulation of notes.

Augmentation. Proportionally lengthening the note values of a melody, or widening an interval by a semitone. For example, a melody in quavers is augmented if it then appears in crotchets; an augmented 5th (F – C♯) is one semitone wider than a perfect 5th (F – C). Opposite of *diminution*.

Augmented triad. A triad formed from two major 3rds, so the outer interval of the chord is an augmented 5th (for example, the chord F, A, C♯).

Bossa nova. A musical style created in the late 1950s in Brazil, developed from samba and influenced by jazz.

Bridge. A short, contrasting passage connecting two larger sections of a piece. In a pop song it usually links the verse to the chorus.

Cadence. A short melodic or harmonic progression at the end of a phrase that creates a sense of resolution or repose. It is usually formed by two successive chords, for example V-I for a perfect cadence (C to F in F major), or IV-I for a plagal cadence (B♭ to F in F major).

Chromatic. Involves notes that do not belong to the diatonic scale of the present key. For example, in D major the notes F♮, A♯ and E♭ are chromatic.

Consonance. Created by sounds that are considered stable (i.e. do not require resolution) and pleasing to listen to. In western harmony consonant intervals include the octave, major 3rd and perfect 5th. Opposite of *dissonance*.

Contrapuntal. Adjective to describe music that uses *counterpoint*.

Contrary motion. Movement of two parts in opposite directions to each other. For example, the right hand on a piano might play C-D-E-F-E-D-C while at the same time the left hand plays C-B-A-G-A-B-C.

Countermelody. A secondary melodic line played at the same time as a more important and prominent melody. Usually occurs in melody-and-accompaniment texture.

Counterpoint. Two or more melodic lines, each one significant in itself, played together at the same time. Similar to polyphony.

Cross-rhythm. A rhythm that temporarily suggests a different metre to the prevailing one.

Diatonic. Involves notes that belong to the major or minor scale of the present key. For example, in G major the notes A, D and F♯ are diatonic.

Diminution. Proportionally shortening the note values of a melody, or reducing an interval by a semitone. For example, a melody in quavers is diminished if it then appears in semiquavers; a diminished 5th (C – F♯) is one semitone smaller than a perfect 5th (C – G). Opposite of *augmentation*.

Dissonance. Created by sounds that are considered unstable, requiring resolution, and harsh or challenging to listen to. In western harmony dissonant intervals include the minor second, major 7th and tritone. Opposite of *consonance*.

EQ. Short for 'equalisation'. Process of adjusting the relative level of frequencies in an audio signal. Originally designed to correct aspects of a recorded sound so it became more 'equal' to the original.

Falsetto. A vocal technique used by men to sing notes higher than those within their normal voice range.

Homophonic. A texture in which two or more parts move together in chords. In contrast to a polyphonic texture, in which the parts are more rhythmically independent and have greater individual melodic interest.

Imitation. In polyphonic music, the repetition of a melodic motif in a different part.

Inversion. (1) In an inverted chord the lowest note heard is not the root. In a first-inversion chord the third becomes the lowest, and in a second-inversion chord the fifth does. For example, a tonic triad of F major in first inversion is A-C-F, and in second inversion is C-A-F.

(2) In an inverted melody rising intervals become falling ones and vice-versa, so the inverted melody looks like a mirror image of the original.

(3) In an inverted interval the lowest note becomes the highest as it is moved up an octave. For example, F-A inverted becomes A-F.

Melisma. One syllable sung to three or more notes.

Modulation. The process of changing key.

Mordent. A quick ornament that goes from the main note to the note above or below and then back again. An upper mordent is indicated by the symbol ✹. A lower mordent is indicated by the symbol ✹.

Multitracking. Recording two or more tracks at the same time. For example members of a string quartet could play together while being recorded onto separate tracks, each of which can be individually modified but still form a cohesive whole.

Orchestration. Refers to the study of the way music is scored for instruments, or the process of scoring music for an orchestra.

Ostinato. A repeating melodic, harmonic or rhythmic motif, heard continuously throughout part or the whole of a piece.

Overdubbing. Recording a new track over the top of previously recorded tracks, resulting in a combined multitrack recording.

Panning. Positioning a recorded sound within the stereo image.

Parallel motion. Movement of two parts in the same direction, with the interval between them remaining consistent. For example, the right hand on a piano might play C-D-F-G-E while at the same time the left hand plays A-B-D-E-C.

Passing note. A non-harmony note placed between and connecting two harmony notes, which are usually a 3rd apart from each other.

Pedal note. A long-held note, usually sustained in a lower register, over which changing harmonies occur.

Pizzicato. A direction to pluck rather than bow notes on a string instrument.

Power chord. A chord comprised of the root and fifth of a triad, played on the electric guitar.

Programme music. Instrumental music that attempts to portray non-musical ideas or images, such as a particular character or landscape.

Riff. A short, catchy melodic figure, repeated as an ostinato and commonly found in rock, pop and jazz.

Rondo. A musical form in which a theme in the tonic key returns regularly throughout a piece, recurrences separated by episodes made up of contrasting material.

Sampler. A device that combines, modifies and plays back recorded sounds known as samples.

Scotch snap. A two-note dotted rhythm which has the shorter note on the beat. Usually an on-beat semiquaver followed by an off-beat dotted quaver. Also known as a lombardic rhythm.

Sequencer. A device used to record, edit and play back sounds stored as MIDI information.

Stop time. A rhythmic device in jazz in which the backing section plays sparsely-spaced chords (usually on the first beat of every bar) separated by periods of silence. Provides a frame for the soloist to improvise over.

Strophic. A song that repeats the same music for different verses. Opposite of *through-composed*.

Syncopation. The displacement of an accent from a strong beat to a weak one, so that off-beat notes become stressed.

Synthesiser. An electronic instrument used to generate and modify a variety of sounds, both musical (such as the imitation of other instruments) and non-musical.

Through-composed. A song in which each verse is set to different music. Opposite of *strophic*.

Timbre. Tone colour. The quality of a note that allows us to distinguish between different instruments. A note of the same pitch, loudness and duration will sound different when played on the clarinet and the trumpet because of their different timbres. Also used to describe more subjectively the tone quality of a particular instrument, for example through words such as 'bright', 'harsh' or 'mellow'.

Transposition. The movement up or down in pitch of a whole passage of music or piece.

Tremolando. The fast and continuous repetition of a single note, creating a trembling effect.

Turn. A four-note ornament that 'turns' around the main note. It starts on the note above, drops to the main note, drops to the note below and then returns to the main note. Indicated by the symbol ∾.

Tutti. A direction for all of the performers in an ensemble (or section) to play together.

Unison. Simultaneous performance of the same note or melody by a number of people.

Variation structure. Consists of a theme which is then repeated and modified a number of times to form variations.

Verse-chorus structure. A song form in which verses alternate with a chorus, to create a structure such as verse-chorus-verse.

Vibraphone. A tuned percussion instrument, similar to the xylophone but larger and with resonators hanging down from each key. The electronically driven resonators are fitted with lids which can rapidly open and close to produce a vibrato effect.

Whole tone. An interval of two semitones, for example A♭-B♭ or E-F♯. A whole-tone scale consists only of whole tones, for example C-D-E-F♯-G♯-A♯.

Word painting. Using music to illustrate certain words or phrases in a song. For example 'jagged mountains' might be represented by an angular melody and 'low plains' by a low register.

Index